GET YAMAMOTO

by Burke Davis

get yamamoto
by burke davis

BANTAM BOOKS
TORONTO · NEW YORK · LONDON
A NATIONAL GENERAL COMPANY

GET YAMAMOTO

*A Bantam Book / published by arrangement with
Random House, Inc.*

PRINTING HISTORY

*Random House edition published June 1969
2nd printing .... July 1969
Military Book Club edition published 1969
Bantam edition published January 1971*

*Bantam Books are published by Bantam Books, Inc., a National
General company. Its trade-mark, consisting of the words "Bantam
Books" and the portrayal of a bantam, is registered in the United
States Patent Office and in other countries. Marca Registrada.
Bantam Books, Inc., 666 Fifth Avenue, New York, N.Y. 10019.*

PRINTED IN THE UNITED STATES OF AMERICA

To the memory of
John Marion Virden, late Colonel, U.S.A.F.

Contents

get yamamoto

1

The Peacock
Flies on Sunday

AT 8:01 A.M., with a brisk rhythmic fall of rubber heels on linoleum, Commander Edwin T. Layton, the fleet intelligence officer at Pearl Harbor, passed along the first-floor corridor of Headquarters bound for his briefing of the Admiral. This morning Layton carried a death warrant in his worn manila folder.

Morning colors had just been sounded and echoes of Navy bugles still hung in the air. Flags had been raised before the building and on ships in the harbor, some five hundred feet below. The fleet and the airfields were busy, and heavy traffic snaked along roads to and from Honolulu; the teeming naval bases of Hawaii had begun the work of another wartime day. It was April 14, 1943.

A little more than sixteen months earlier Japanese planes had struck here, plunging the United States into war—a strike launched by Admiral Isoroku Yamamoto, the most daring and formidable of Japan's naval strategists. Now Yamamoto, Commander in Chief of the Japanese Combined Fleet, was to move into a combat zone for the first time—perhaps within reach of American planes. Secret word of his movement was among Layton's briefing papers today.

Layton had served in Tokyo as early as 1929, had become friendly with many Japanese military and political leaders, and spoke and read Japanese expertly. He knew Yamamoto well, and realized that he had seldom carried a more urgent intelligence matter to Admiral Nimitz.

Layton passed a Marine sentry posted outside the Admiral's suite and nodded. A sign above the outer door read:

"Nations, like men, should grasp time by the forelock instead of the fetlock."

The Admiral was given to the use of pointed maxims.

On one wall, under glass, hung a Samurai sword taken from the body of the commander of a Japanese midget submarine sunk off Pearl Harbor on December 7, 1941.

The commander and the flag lieutenant in the outer office exchanged the same words they had used each morning, month after month, like actors in a play written in Navy argot.

"Zero Zero is in, and will see you now," the aide said. It was 8:02 A.M. Layton was on time. He entered the office of Admiral Chester W. Nimitz, Commander in Chief, Pacific Fleet and Pacific Ocean Areas. Nimitz gave him a friendly greeting in his soft Texas drawl.

Layton sat, as he invariably did, in a chair against the wall at the Admiral's left, with a window behind him opening onto the blank concrete wall of Zero Zero's pistol range and tennis backboard. The office was so still that the footfalls of the Marine sentry in the corridor could be heard. The room was oddly reminiscent of a Hawaiian cottage on some Navy row in the hills. Drapes of a gaudy, flowered print matched the chairs of split bamboo—furnishings left behind by evacuated Navy families and now put to use at Headquarters. The Admiral's desk was cluttered with souvenir ashtrays. Under the glass top were several stern mottoes and a signed photograph of General Douglas MacArthur.

Layton handed Nimitz the text of an intercepted Japanese message, freshly decoded and translated by Communications Intelligence. "Our old friend Yamamoto," he said.

Nimitz pursed his wide mouth with an expression of anticipation as he began to read. He sat rigidly erect and looked lean and fit. He had been up for two hours or more, and had hiked a couple of miles in the hills before breakfast. The Admiral passed a hand through his thinning sun-bleached hair. One finger of the left hand was missing, the result of an accident with the Navy's first diesel engine, which Nimitz had built long ago. He scanned the sheets of the enemy dispatch rapidly.

Through the window behind the Admiral, Layton saw the green cliffside at the foot of the extinct volcano Makalapa, and far below, the northern reaches of Pearl Harbor, the oil tanks and a tip of Ford Island, still showing few reminders of the swarming Japanese bombers and torpedo planes. Beyond his view, the rusting upper works of the ruined *Arizona* still thrust above the water.

A memory of prewar Japan flashed into Layton's mind as Nimitz read, a glimpse of a raw, misty autumn day in 1937 at the Emperor's hunting preserve, when Isoroku Yamamoto had played host on a duck hunt to a party of naval officers, Japanese, American, British and Dutch. Layton could still almost smell the rich odors of soy sauce and ginger and wild duck that had boiled up from the sukiyaki pans. They had caught the ducks as they flew from a canal, trapping them in long-handled nets as Yamamoto laughed and shouted encouragement above the honking and flapping of the terrified birds. It was a Yamamoto Layton had never seen, charming, friendly, courteous and dignified. He presided over the serving dishes to urge generous portions upon each guest, a short, trim, athletic figure striding about with bottles of sake and Old Parr Scotch, barking hospitably, "Drink up! Drink up! Good friends must be kept warm." Layton had played bridge against the Admiral, who played with skill and confidence; Yamamoto had won both rubbers. At the hunt's end, with ceremonial care, the Admiral had presented each officer with some of the Emperor's ducks.

CHESTER NIMITZ read the intercepted enemy message Layton had brought, a detailed itinerary of Yamamoto's movements in the South Pacific islands, some four thousand miles from Honolulu:

The inspection tour of the Commander in Chief Combined Fleet to Ballale, Shortland and Buin on April 18 is scheduled as follows:

0600 depart Rabaul by medium attack plane (accompanied by six fighters).

0800 arrive Ballale. Depart immediately for Shortland by subchaser (1st Base Force will prepare one boat), arriving Shortland 0840.

0945 depart Shortland by subchaser, arriving Ballale 1030. (For transportation, prepare assault boat at Shortland and motor launch at Ballale.)

1100 depart Ballale by medium attack plane arriving Buin

*1110. Lunch at Headquarters, 1st Base Force. (Senior Staff
Officer, Air Flotilla 26, to be present.)*

*1400 depart Buin by medium attack plane, arriving Rabaul
1540 . . .*

*In the event of inclement weather, there will be a post-
ponement of one day.*

April 18 would be Sunday. Four days away. This revelation
of the hour-by-hour movements of a key Japanese commander presented a rare opportunity. If Yamamoto kept to his
schedule he would be vulnerable. It remained only to devise
an attack.

Nimitz smiled slightly. "What do you say? Do we try to
get him?" His bright blue eyes darkened in his tanned face.
The Admiral was already studying a wall chart of the South
Pacific, glancing along the island barrier that lay above
Australia, a green chain looping down to the northeast of
New Guinea, stretching more than a thousand miles from the
Bismarcks to the Solomons—the front where he had sent
Admiral William F. Halsey to face Yamamoto.

Years later, Layton would have a vivid recollection of
these moments, and though unable to reconstruct the exact
words of the entire interview, he never forgot the calm
discussion in which the death of Yamamoto was ordered.
Layton began:

"Assuming that we have planes able to intercept him—it
would have to be planes—you should first consider, I suppose,
what would be gained by killing him.

"He's unique among their people. He's the one Jap who
thinks in bold strategic terms—in that way more American
than Japanese. The younger officers and enlisted men idolize
him. Aside from the Emperor, probably no man in Japan is so
important to civilian morale. And if he's shot down, it would
demoralize the fighting Navy. You know the Japanese psy-
chology; it would stun the nation."

Nimitz agreed. "The one thing that concerns me is whether
they could find a more effective fleet commander."

They discussed several four-star Japanese admirals, men
known to them for years; Layton outlined their professional
competence, experience, personalities and outlook. "Yamamoto is head and shoulders above them all, as you know."

"Yes, all right. Anything else?"

"No, sir. I'm sure it's sound doctrine to strike at the heart of the enemy, and I say this is a chance. I believe that's good Clausewitz. Yamamoto is certainly a symbol of their first victories, here and Wake and the Dutch Indies and Burma."

"If we kill him, would the Japs take some kind of revenge—put on more strikes?"

"We know they're straining harder every day," Layton said. "They're scraping the bottom of the barrel for fighter pilots and all air group people. We've got them reacting to our attacks now. I can't see them putting on new offensives."

Nimitz responded almost absently, his tranquil gaze still on the chart. "It wouldn't do our own morale any harm. Think of how it would cheer up Halsey and Mitscher. They took Pearl Harbor as a personal affront, and they've been living for the day they can pay 'em back in spades. . . It's down in Halsey's bailiwick. If there's a way, he'll find it. All right, we'll try it."

Nimitz had an afterthought: "Is there a danger we'd compromise the code break with this one, and pay for it later on?"

"We shouldn't leave it to chance," Layton said. "Why not have all personnel involved briefed with a cover story? We could say it came from Australian coastwatchers around Rabaul. Everybody in the Pacific thinks they're miracle men."

Nimitz drew out a pad and wrote a dispatch for Halsey at Noumea, in New Caledonia, Headquarters, South Pacific, giving him details of Yamamoto's forthcoming flight from Rabaul to Bougainville, and adding; "If forces your command have capability intercept and shoot down Yamamoto and staff, you are hereby authorized initiate preliminary planning."

"Let's leave the details to Halsey," Nimitz said. "He'll have four days to get ready. He'll need 'em."

AT FIVE MINUTES BEFORE SIX O'CLOCK on the afternoon of April 13, only fourteen hours earlier, a monitor at nearby Wahiawa radio station began taking an enciphered message in Japanese. He was one of the nameless men of FRUPAC (Fleet Radio Unit, Pacific Fleet) who listened constantly, through three daily shifts, to the chattering of Japanese operators from the western and southern Pacific. This message of 5:55 was one among hundreds. At first, there was no sign that the most extraordinary interception of the war had begun, an achievement of the code-breakers of Naval Intelligence.

The distant Japanese operator had hardly signed off before his message appeared in Combat Intelligence headquarters at Pearl Harbor. The Navy monitor at Wahiawa used an ingenious typewriter with the "Kana" keyboard in Japanese, which simultaneously cut a teletype tape: this tape, in turn, was fed into a transmitter and sent automatically to Combat Intelligence. The intelligence den was in a cellar guarded by sentries and steel vault doors, the domain of a talented band of code-crackers whose code name was Hypo. Men in the cellar worked over the intercepted message throughout the night of April 13–14.

The message from Wahiawa appeared in a room loud with the clamor of IBM tabulating machines, where operators transferred the Japanese coded numerals onto their punch cards, fed these into the machines, which whirred and clattered and at length tapped out new versions of the message, now decoded plain text in Japanese.

The electrical code-crackers had an awesome reputation in the upper echelons of the Navy—a secret weapon which had helped to win the battle of Midway, reading Japanese orders with such accuracy that American carrier commanders had been able to intercept the enemy with a stealthy approach of their own. The noisy robots were the creatures of Lieutenant Commander Thomas H. Dyer, an Annapolis graduate who had taken up cryptanalysis as a hobby, had devised ways to speed the laborious task of decoding manually, and had become the father of machine cryptanalysis.

Today Dyer's machines had been prepared with the key to the current version of the most widely used of the Japanese Navy's high-security codes, known to Americans as JN 25. It was a complex code of some 45,000 five-digit groups, devised to be put into cipher with the use of 100,000 "additives," also of five digits each. The solution to this code system had been worked out over the past three years by Navy groups scattered from Washington to the Philippines, and had been kept up to date despite periodic changes in the code. The information stored in the IBM machines on this Tuesday evening was so complete as to include additives introduced by the enemy less than two weeks before, on April 1.*

The decoded messages went from the IBM room to the traffic analysts, one of whom thumbed through the sheafs of enemy dispatches, noted that the one of 5:55 P.M. bore an unusual number of addressees, and flagged it for attention. He routed the message to Lieutenant Colonel Alva Bryan Lasswell of the Marine Corps, a veteran of the translation section who had been a language officer in Tokyo for three years before the war. The translation went rapidly.

The plain text was almost complete as it came from the machine, but Lasswell filled in a few blanks and called for help from Tom Dyer and his assistant, Lieutenant Commander Wesley Wright. Dyer, who made use of the mysterious recesses of the machines as if they were extensions of his brain, provided several additives to the code, making the message fuller. "Ham" Wright, a burly red-haired man who had been in cryptology almost as long as Dyer, identified the code symbols for several place names—islands and bases in the Solomon Islands chain:

RR meant *Rabaul,* a key Japanese base; RXZ was *Ballale,* and RXE was *Shorthand,* small islands off Bougainville; RXP was *Buin,* a base on Bougainville. With this aid, Lasswell completed his translation, a concise message detailing the movements of Yamamoto from Rabaul to Bougainville and return for the coming Sunday.

---

* The United States had been reading Japanese codes since 1920, when the erratic genius Herbert O. Yardley worked miracles with his "Black Chamber." Despite Yardley's published revelations of breaks, many Japanese experts considered their later machine codes unassailable. Yardley's "break," they insisted, had been accomplished by the theft of code books.

In 1926, in an equally important achievement, an unsung Washington cryptanalyst known to history only as "Miss Aggie" had cracked the Japanese Admirals' code, which was used for the most sensitive traffic. The American services, particularly the Navy, had monitored Japanese military and diplomatic traffic in all the years since, including the months prior to the attack on Pearl Harbor.

As recently as January, 1943, a large Japanese submarine, the I-1, with thousands of code books aboard, had been forced aground on Guadalcanal by the New Zealand corvette *Kiwi;* valuable additives captured there were in use by intelligence at Pearl Harbor in April 1943, as the Yamamoto mission developed.

The dispatch bore the signature of Vice Admiral Tomoshige, commander of the Japanese 8th Fleet, with headquarters at Shortland, an island off the southern tip of Bougainville. Lasswell recognized the Admiral as a newcomer to the South Pacific theater; until lately Samejima had served as naval aide to Emperor Hirohito in Tokyo.

Lasswell looked at a calender. This one was perishable. It wouldn't keep for long. Someone would be thinking of evening old scores. He hurried his final copy to Commander Layton.

DURING THE NIGHT OF APRIL 14 Nimitz had a reply from Vice Admiral Theodore S. (Ping) Wilkinson, Halsey's executive officer at Noumea, in New Caledonia. Halsey was in Australia for a few days. In his absence Wilkinson had determined that the operation was feasible. Vice Admiral Marc ("Pete") Mitscher, commander of a combined air force in the Solomon Islands said that P-38's from Guadalcanal could handle the mission. Plans were being made in Halsey's absence.

Nimitz and Layton conferred on Yamamoto once more at the morning briefing of April 15, and positive orders went out. Nimitz added a final personal note to Halsey: "Good luck and good hunting." The mission was on.

Nimitz was in a good humor at the end of this briefing. He shot on the pistol range at noon, challenging younger officers to a match, and later in the afternoon he was off in his battleship-gray jeep, USS Hush-Hush, a gift from the Army. His driver took him far beyond the crowds at Waikiki, where barbed-wire barricades were hung with towels and wet clothing, and Nimitz plunged into the sea for his regular one-mile swim. He was soon back at his desk, in his quiet way perfecting plans that would push the war westward through the 65 million square miles of his domain. Nimitz was an unassuming, tireless man who made no display of his dedication and relentless will. His office, one of the staff had said lately, was surely the most efficient military establishment in the world, and it operated with only the rarest hints of stress. Nimitz recited for some of his staff a few more of his gamy maxims about why battleships were classed as feminine, and played cribbage after supper.

THE SECRET was not Pearl Harbor's alone. By April 15 guarded rumors of the Yamamoto mission were heard in Washington, where they inspired gossip and legends that would persist for many years. The enemy Admiral's itinerary had been picked up by a Navy radioman in a bunker, at Dutch Harbor, Alaska, above whom seven radio masts towered three hundred feet into the chilly fog. The coded message had then been relayed to Pearl Harbor and to Washington. Cryptanalysts and translators in the capital, working simultaneously with those in Hawaii, had bared its secrets within five hours. Intelligence operatives in Pearl Harbor and Washington were soon exchanging information about the Yamamoto mission, even additives to the decoded message as they were worked out. One day after Admiral Nimitz learned of the intercepted message, the news was taken to Frank Knox, the aging veteran of Theodore Roosevelt's Rough Riders who was Secretary of the Navy. The Yamamoto affair moved through the Secretary's hands without leaving a trace of its passage on his office log.

Frank Knox lived on the Navy's yacht, *Sequoia*, moored in the Potomac. On April 15, as he did each morning, the Secretary rose at six thirty, climbed the river bluff to Fort Washington, took a brisk walk, jogged back to the boat for his calisthenics, a shower, massage and a gargantuan breakfast. By eight o'clock he emerged, with his ruddy face aglow and eyes sparkling behind rimless pince-nez, to be driven to his office. He was sixty-nine but looked ten years younger.

Knox entered his office and began dealing with the affairs of the day. One of his first callers was an unrecorded visitor, Captain Ellis M. Zacharias, Deputy Chief of Naval Intelligence, who briefed him on the Yamamoto matter. The details of their conference and its consequences were never to be revealed. Zacharias described Yamamoto's flight plans for Palm Sunday and urged that the Japanese Admiral be killed. According to one version of a story which seeped from his office, the Secretary had thought it a trifling matter until, over lunch with a few officers, he fell to talking of ancient wars, when individual champions had been sent out to meet in personal combat. Knox thought then of Yamamoto. Should he be shot down? Was there precedent for the assassination of enemy leaders in war-time?

The Secretary also called General Henry H. Arnold, Chief of the Army Air Forces. Arnold was enthusiastic. Certainly, he said, Yamamoto should be shot down if he came within reach. Knox and Arnold had sought expert advice. It was at this point that gossip began to embellish the story with inaccuracies. Arnold, it was said, had called in Charles Lindbergh for counsel on long-range flights by P-38's, and Lindbergh, in turn, had called Frank Meyer of Lockheed, who had nursed the big twin-engine Lightning fighter almost from birth.

In fact, Lindbergh was not in Washington, and he was to learn of the Yamamoto mission only afterward; the famous aviator was not acquainted with Frank Meyer.

One report was based on fact: Knox had taken the problem to President Franklin D. Roosevelt and got his approval for the mission.

Roosevelt had left Washington by train on April 13 for a tour of military bases in the South and West, and spent the next three nights in Georgia and Alabama. His official log showed no call from Knox in this time, and their last recorded personal meeting had been on March 24. Their contacts concerning Yamamoto were deliberately omitted from the record.

And yet, as a handful of men in Washington knew, several offices in the higher reaches of government were abuzz with plans to kill Yamamoto.

Lieutenant Commander Charles N. Spinks, a language specialist who had served in Japan until shortly before Pearl Harbor, was in charge of the Japanese desk in a division of Naval Intelligence called OP-16-FE. In these mid-April days Spinks handled heavy traffic between Washington and Pearl Harbor about the Yamamoto affair, most of it "on the political side." Spinks knew nothing of the origin of the plan, except that an intercepted message was involved, but he assumed that the decision was being made in Washington, because so much of the traffic was originating there, and "since there were such important political and psychological aspects involved."

It was clear to Spinks that plans were being made, since other intelligence officers working on the case frequently called on him for advice on precise shades of meaning in the Japanese text. Spinks got the impression, as he completed his work on the matter, that both Washington and Pearl Harbor had a hand in making the decision.

Admiral William C. Mott, a communications specialist, was on duty in the White House map room, and made up daily composite dispatches of interesting war news and sent it to military and naval aids aboard the Presidential train, to be passed on to Roosevelt. Mott sent word of the Yamamoto mission to the train, though so far as he knew, FDR took no active part in the decision. "He left such things with the military," Mott said. As a matter of fact, an order invoking the President's authority was being prepared for dispatch to the South Pacific. The order was signed by Frank Knox.

During the hurried two or three days of discussion, scores of messages passed between Pearl Harbor and Washington; there was no question of granting Nimitz "permission" to order the assassination in his theater. Almost everyone was agreed. As Admiral Samuel Eliot Morison later wrote, Nimitz had put a simple question to Washington: "Would the elimination of Yamamoto help our cause? . . . Did Japan have anyone as good or better to take his place? To the latter, the intelligence answer was a decided 'No!' "

It remained only to convince Frank Knox, and it was Captain Zacharias who had won his support. In the process, the Captain gave other officers a fascinating glimpse into the flurry of activity in the Yamamoto case, as the decision was being made.

Zacharias' office was in Building L, a shabby "temporary" building in the Navy compound on the mall, a highly restricted area guarded by trigger-happy Marine veterans back from Guadalcanal, who were said to fire at ghostly Japanese figures in the reflection pool at night. In one end of the building Admiral Morison and his numerous crew of historians were writing their story of the Navy at war.

In another section of L was a singular branch of intelligence known as Special Warfare Activities. Its chief of research was Ladislas Farago, a veteran Hungarian newspaper correspondent who had seen most of the opening moves of World War II in Europe, from Ethiopia to the fall of Poland. Though he was an enemy alien, he was deep in U.S. intelligence work. "We weren't really intelligence," he remembered, "but mischief makers. We planned sabotage against the enemy—mostly pin pricks, to irritate and bedevil them."

Special Warfare set afloat wild rumors through spies, sent false broadcasts to German U-boats—and once in a master stroke carried biological warfare to the German Navy by planting girls with fresh cases of venereal disease in the bordellos of Marseille.

On April 15 Zacharias entered the office in Building L where, as deputy chief, he directed the affairs of Naval Intelligence. He was a veteran of many years of counter-espionage against Japan, and had dueled with a succession of spies in Washington since 1920.

No one in the United States knew more about Isoroku Yamamoto than Ellis Zacharias.

The Captain could not conceal his excitement this morning. As he paced his office with a sheaf of papers in his hand, Farago detected his condition: "He looked like he had eaten of canary—he was obviously pregnant with a tremendous secret. He looked as if he had to do something or explode."

Zacharias beckoned Farago outside, into a courtyard behind the building. They walked slowly beside the reflecting pool as Zacharias unburdened himself.

"Frank Knox is a mystery to me," he said. "He has a chance to shoot down Yamamoto, but he has qualms—and he's looking for a precedent. It defies the imagination." He held his papers out to Farago, a report from the Navy's Judge Advocate General on the legalities of the planned assassination. Zacharias complained that some officers feared Drew Pearson and a committee investigation more than the Japanese Navy.

Farago glanced over the brief report from Admiral Woodson: since the Japanese had bombed Pearl Harbor and the Philippines in sneak attacks without a declaration of war, they were outlaws among nations, and had forfeited the protection of international law.

Zacharias asked Farago to prepare a list of precedents for killing enemy leaders in wartime, speaking with unusual insistance: "We've got to be sure they get him. He's the most dangerous man we face in the Pacific."

"How about Leopold the Third?" Farago said. "The Germans snatched him up. And how about Napoleon the Third, merely kidnapped and held prisoner. And then there was some Hungarian king, killed in battle in 1526—murdered, you might say."

"Good," the Captain said. "Any more?"

"Not out of the top of my head. Give me time and we'll sink them with precedent."

"There's no time" Zacharias said. "Write me a memo as soon as you can and I'll take it to Knox myself." He returned to the Secretary's office, alone, carrying Farago's list of precedents for assassination in wartime.

FAR OUT IN THE SOUTH PACIFIC, dispatches on the Yamamoto mission passing between American command posts grew more urgent. On April 16, two days after Nimitz had made his decision, Bull Halsey sent one to Marc Mitscher at Guadalcanal, who was beginning his third week as Commander Air, Solomon Islands.

Mitscher read the message in his headquarters beside the swift Lunga River, within sight of his crude fighter strips and Henderson Field. He was sweltering under canvas and slapping at mosquitoes; his desk was the top of a battered footlocker.

The dispatch was couched in Halsey's droll style. IT AP-PEARS THE PEACOCK WILL BE ON TIME. FAN HIS TAIL.

Pete Mitscher had a day and a half.

2

The Quarry

IT WAS 1:30 A.M. OF DECEMBER 8, 1941, in the Imperial Fleet's home anchorage on the Inland Sea. Aboard the flagship *Yamato*, men had been waiting all night for news that war had begun.

Isoroku Yamamoto sat unobtrusively in a corner in his folding chair, eyes half closed, almost motionless, as if deaf to the nervous whispers of his staff; a swart, muscular little man whose dress uniform was wrinkled by a night of waiting. An aura of Hechima cologne hung about him. He was fifty-seven years old, but despite the gray at his temples, might have passed for forty-five.

The three fingers of his maimed left hand drummed lightly on the chair now and then, but the strong, somber face was unchanged. Captain Yasuji Watanabe, the fleet landing operations officer, thought that Yamamoto was the calmest man in the operations room of the *Yamato* at this moment. The impassive Commander in Chief of the Combined Fleet, Imperial Japanese Navy, was launching a war that would take the lives of 400,000 Americans and 1,220,000 Japanese.

In Hawaii, 3000 miles to the east, it was 6 A.M., December 7. Not far north of Pearl Harbor a Japanese task force of twenty-three ships was launching its planes on a strike against the American base. It was this fleet, still under radio silence, from which Isoroku Yamamoto awaited word.

Yamamoto's operations room was flooded in light. Senior officers leaned over a large chart, studying waters around the Hawaiian Islands, where Vice Admiral Chuichi Nagumo's task force should be now. Admiral Shigeru Fukudome, the chief of naval operations, who had until recently been Yamamoto's chief of staff, kept watch over the others and made mental notes for his diary. The officers glanced often at the small brass Navy clock on the bulkhead. Yamamoto looked as if he were falling asleep.

"It's about time," someone said. The officers on the flagship had visions of the carrier planes taking off in the darkness, so far away.

They had almost two hours of waiting, in the flagship in the Hashirojima anchorage, before the first word of the outcome of the attack on Pearl Harbor. Soon they would know whether Nagumo had surprised the enemy. For Yamamoto there had been a lifetime of preparation for a war he had resisted—but for which he had built a new kind of fighting force.

THE GEISHA called him Eighty Sen.

Two fingers were missing from his left hand, a wound he had borne as a badge of honor since the battle of Tsushima, when Admiral Togo had destroyed the Russian fleet. And so the giggling geisha reduced the price of a manicure when Isoroku Yamamoto came: "Ten fingers, one yen—eight fingers, eighty sen."

The maimed hand was a totem of the Admiral's austere life, it was seldom out of his mind. Long ago, at the birth of his first son, Yamamoto had been strangely withdrawn and diffident, but finally expressed his anxiety to his mother-in-law: "His hand—the boy's hand. Has he five fingers?" Laughing in relief, he had become the proud father of convention, ridiculing himself: "Common sense told me he must have all his fingers, but still . . ."

The Navy and foreign diplomats knew him as a distinguished Japanese naval officer, impeccable in dress and unfailingly, almost embarrassingly, courteous; intimates found him emotional, moved by strong likes and dislikes, naïve, boyish and mischievous. In younger days he had been renowned for dramatic entrances to geisha houses and naval quarters afloat—stepping within and pitching forward to stand on his head, immobile, in a show of controlled strength. He also frequently performed a peasant dance, a frenzied jig accompanied by the skilled balancing of plates above his head.

He had been born in a remote village in northwest Japan,

the son of a schoolmaster, Sadakichi Takano, who had given him the unusual name Isoroku—"Fifty-Six"—to commemorate the age of the father at the boy's birth on April 4, 1884. Isoroku had survived a rigorous boyhood, was trained in sports and military maneuvers in Nagaoka Middle School, where he also learned English from an American missionary; from his father he learned Chinese calligraphy, an art he was to cherish all his life.

He had been an unpredictable child. Once, in the home of a friend, his hostess watched him gulp his food in wonder. "Isoroku, I believe you could eat anything—nothing would be safe from your appetite, except perhaps this pencil." Isoroku said nothing, but the woman was soon startled by the sound of the boy crunching the wooden pencil. She watched incredulously as he stoically swallowed its brittle remains. At sixteen, finishing second among three hundred applicants in his entrance examinations, Isoroku entered the Japanese Naval Academy at Etajima, a spartan institution whose cadets cruised for a year on a windjammer, and each summer were forced to make an exhausting ten-mile marathon swim which took a toll of a tenth of them. Isoroku had hardly finished the academy when Japan delivered a sneak attack on Russian ships at Port Arthur in 1904 and opened the war which made her a world power. Isoroku fought under Admiral Togo at the battle of Tsushima, as a boy ensign on the cruiser *Nisshin,* and had written his family:

> When the shells began to fly above me, I found I was not afraid . . . A shell hit the *Nisshin* and knocked me unconscious. When I recovered I found I was wounded in the right leg and two fingers of my left hand were missing . . . But when victory was announced at 2 A.M. even the wounded cheered.

After the war, when his parents died, Isoroku was adopted, by the wealthy Yamamoto family of Nagaoka, in a tradition much more common in Japan than in the West; he assumed the Yamamoto name. Isoroku was also married in his native region to Reiko Mihashi, the rather plain daughter of a local dairy farmer; four children were born to them.

The passion of Yamamoto's life was gambling; he was the Navy champion at *go* and *shogi,* games similar to checkers and chess, and played Western games, poker and bridge, with fierce concentration.

Isoroku was a stubborn and unorthodox man, but in a tradition-bound navy his rise was meteoric. Like Billy Mitchell in the United States, he had an early vision of military aviation. In 1915 he told an American reporter, "The most important warship of the future will be a ship to carry airplanes." At the end of the World War he spent two years at Harvard, pursuing two subjects, oil and American planes, with such application that several American oil companies offered him jobs. He already planned naval battles in the air.

Back home, Yamamoto became a leader in the building of a naval air force. In 1923 he became director of a new air training school at Kasumigaura, where he took the entire course of instruction with his students—theory, gunnery, communications and flying lessons as well. He won the attention of his students by insisting that he make a cross-country flight with the poorest pilot among them, and won their hearts by running with them in the school marathon race and finishing second, though the boys were only half his age.

Yamamoto was a stern master; he persisted in drilling pilots in night flying despite many casualties—saying that wars were won by surprise attacks, and that Japanese airmen must fly by day and night. He did not forbid his pilots to drink, and often sent sake to their rooms, though he drank only tea himself. He explained, "I haven't drunk since I was commissioned. I found I wasn't strong in the head and made a fool of myself, so I stopped."

By 1925 Yamamoto was back in America, as naval attaché in Washington, this time assigned to study American defense industries. Many Japanese attachés had come spying before him in the U.S. capital, but none like Yamamoto. Captain Ellis Zacharias, who became his adversary, recognized the change: "His predecessors had concentrated on information of a tactical nature: techniques of gunnery, details of our vessels, battle order ... Now, it seemed, the naval attaché's office was no longer interested in tactical and technical data. Suddenly operational problems of highest strategy shifted to the Japanese shopping list. Tactical matters were assigned to lower echelons. The naval attaché was interested in greater things; he was interested in war ... The aircraft carrier, the combination of sea power and air power, was an obsession with Yamamoto ... I always felt that the first plans for the Pearl Harbor attack originated in his restless brain right here in Washington."

The Captain returned to Japan in 1926 with a low opinion of his future enemies. He once told an American correspondent, "The American Navy is a social navy of bridge and golf players. A peacetime navy." He turned to the building of a very different kind of navy. By 1927 Japan already had four aircraft carriers; her swift destroyers were ten to fifteen years in advance of their time, with five-inch guns such as were not to appear on American ships until the middle of World War II. In this growing navy many innovations could be traced to Yamamoto, who served as chief of the technical division of the bureau of aeronautics, then as chief of the bureau.

The London Naval Conference of 1934 made Yamamoto a hero. As chief of his delegation, he was determined to break the ratio of battleships permitted by treaty—five-five-three in favor of the U.S. and England over Japan—a ratio he branded "national degradation." This ratio had been forced upon Japan at the Washington Disarmament Conference of 1921 by the United States, whose diplomats were emboldened by the fact that they were reading the Japanese code. The Americans realized that though the Orientals could not publicly accept inferiority at sea, they had resigned themselves to this ratio. The American code break was still unknown to the Japanese, these thirteen years later.

Early in 1934 Yamamoto crossed the United States by train on his way to London. He rode in a locked compartment, playing all-night poker games with his companions and declining to see reporters. He once broke silence to scoff at the thought of a Japanese-American war, which Billy Mitchell was then forecasting to congressional committees.

Yamamoto gave bland assurances: "I do not regard relations between the United States and Japan from the same angle as General Mitchell. I have never thought of America as a potential enemy, and the naval plans of Japan have never included the possibility of a Japanese-American war." In London, Yamamoto told reporters who met him at the dock, "Japan can no longer submit to the ratio system. There is no possibility of compromise by my government on that point." For more than two months, through rounds of exhausting talks, he insisted that Japan would no longer be bound by restrictive treaties.

His manner at the conference table was warm and friendly, though the Anglo-Americans did not budge from their position, but one delegate, Sanwa, long remembered Yamamoto's impassioned words in private: "If we wait long enough, there will come a day when we can smash the Americans and English." There was an undiplomatic light in his eye.

The conference ended without agreement. The old treaty was in ruins and Japan was free to build the navy she wanted.

Yamamoto's delegation returned in triumph to Tokyo, to be led in a street procession of two thousand admirals and members of the nationalist societies to the palace, where the Emperor congratulated the victor of London.

While he was being lionized in Tokyo, Yamamoto fell in love with a geisha, Chioko Kawai, a reigning queen of the Navy's clandestine social life. He saw her first at a party in an expensive geisha house in the district of Tsukiki. The girl watched his clumsy efforts to twist the cover from a lacquered soup bowl with his maimed hand, and wounded his vanity by moving to help him. He rejected her brusquely: "Leave me alone. I can do it quite well for myself." She was so angry that she dared her employer's wrath by leaving the party.

A few nights later Chioko met Isoroku once more, introduced to him by an admiral who predicted the Yamamoto would some day become a marshal: "Be nice to him," the admiral said. "Before we know it, this man will be our greatest commander, a *Gensui*."

"He looks more like a country yokel to me." Chioko said. Yamamoto collapsed in laughter; it was his fancy to depict himself as a naïve country boy, groping his way through the labyrinths of sinful Tokyo. Chioko was soon giggling at the little man's laughter, then roaring at his peasant's dance and his astonishing trick of standing on his head. Thus began a romance that was to endure for the eight years of life left to him.

Yamamoto's London triumph became a reality a few months later. Japan advised the U.S. and England that she no longer accepted the naval treaty; in shipyards now screened by high fences the keel of the *Yamato*, first of the four super-battleships, was laid down. Yamamoto remained outwardly friendly to Americans, mingled socially with U.S. naval officers, and courteously received their complaints in a series of incidents—the Marco Polo Bridge incident, the rape of Nanking and other Chinese cities, the "accidental" bombing of the *Panay*, the bombing of U.S. missionary schools, hospitals and oil installations in China, the disappearance of Amelia Earhart among Japanese mandate islands.

Within the Navy Yamamoto pressed for new carriers, and two thirty-four-knot, 30,000 ton monsters, *Shokaku* and *Zuikaku*, were soon on the way. The navy of his dreams was coming into being, but the admirals were not all-powerful, and could not direct the course of events in Japan. The Navy, not yet ready for war, was pushed aside by Army cliques, especially by leaders of the Kwantung Army, who had developed an appetite for conquest in China.

Since 1936 the armed forces had held absolute veto power in national affairs, and by 1939 the more aggressive Army, already embarked on the Chinese adventure, urged that Japan join Germany and Italy in a world war. Like most naval officers, Yamamoto opposed the signing of an Axis pact. He was by no means a pacifist, but he feared that the Army's ignorance of American military power could be disastrous. The Army, in complete control of the press through censorship, and insulated from criticism, moved toward war; Yamamoto spoke out in resistance, though he pushed the Navy relentlessly to prepare it for battle.

In 1940 Prince Fuminaro Konoye formed a new cabinet and signed the Axis pact with Germany and Italy, a step that seemed to make a clash with the United States inevitable. The Minister called in Yamamoto for a conference on the prospects. The Admiral said the Navy was not prepared:

> If I am told to fight regardless of consequences, I shall run wild for the first six months or a year, but for the second and third years I have utterly no confidence.
>
> The Tripartite Pact has been signed and we cannot help it. Now that the situation has come to this pass, I hope you will endeavor to avoid a war with America.

Yamamoto wrote Ryoichi Sasakawa, the leader of the all-Japan Labor Class Federation, a letter whose echoes were to be heard after the Admiral's death a prophetic warning of war to the finish:

> . . . it embarrasses me not a little to hear you say that you "feel at ease in the knowledge that Yamamoto is out at sea

with his fleet." All that I am doing is to devote my utmost, both day and night, toward building up our strength, ever bearing in mind the Imperial admonition:

"Despise not an enemy because he is weak: fear him not because he is strong."

Should hostilities once break out between Japan and the United States, it is not enough that we take Guam and the Philippines, nor even Hawaii and San Francisco. We would have to march into Washington and sign the treaty in the White House. I wonder if our politicians (who speak so lightly of a Japanese-American war) have confidence as to the outcome and are prepared to make the necessary sacrifices.*

When the Navy learned that the Shinpati, a rightist society known as the Soldiers of God, had placed Yamamoto on its assassination list, bodyguards were forced upon him, and Navy Minister Yonai then rushed him to sea as Commander in Chief of the Combined Fleet, a post in which he would be safe from assassins. This was the Navy's highest honor.

Yamamoto had two years to prepare the fleet for its trial. In its first sea exercises the new chief saw that the fleet air arm had only begun to learn its trade, but he was planning strategically as well as improving the readiness of the fleet. Since 1909 the Navy had worked on plans for an American war, based on a strategy of waiting for the enemy to invade the western Pacific, and trapping it with superior maneuvers and gunnery; the Navy had been designed for that war. A few months after he took over the fleet, Yamamoto had moved his frontier defense eastward, on a line through the Marshall Islands, committing the Navy to a more aggressive strategy.

Long training made dramatic improvements in the readiness of the fleet. When Yamamoto took it to sea for maneu-

---

* This letter was to be distorted by Japanese propagandists in a broadcast ten days after Pearl Harbor, in an effort to bolster the morale of the Japanese people, shocked by the unexpected war with America. In that version, long accepted at face value by infuriated Americans, Yamamoto was misquoted:

"Any time war breaks out between Japan and the United States I shall not be content merely to capture Guam and the Philippines and to occupy Hawaii and San Francisco. I am looking forward to dictating peace to the United States at the White House in Washington."

vers in April and May, 1940, torpedo planes bored in on the zig-zagging carriers and battleships so tenaciously that referees ruled half the fleet out of action. Yamamoto watched the end of the exercises from the *Yamato* with the Admiral Shigeru Fukudome of his staff. "It looks as if no fleet can protect itself against torpedo planes," Fukudome said. "Has the time come when decisive battles will be won with aerial torpedoes?"

Yamamoto gave him a thoughtful look. "Have you ever thought that an even more crushing blow could be struck against an unsuspecting fleet?"

Yamamoto did not mention torpedo attacks again until there was news from Italy that British planes had sunk three Italian battleships at anchor in Taranto. He asked Japanese naval attachés in Rome and London for detailed reports. About a month later, in December, 1940, Yamamoto surprised Fukudome: "An air attack on Pearl Harbor might be feasible now—especially since our training goes so well." It was his first mention of a blow at the U.S. Pacific Fleet base.

Yamamoto was in earnest: "I want you to find me a man to plan this. Get me a senior officer, a flier whose past career has not influenced him in conventional operations. I want a study of all aspects of the fleet aerial torpedo problem—and keep this from everyone else, all the fleet staff, everyone."

Fukudome suggested Rear Admiral Takijuro Ohnishi, the Navy's leading aerial philosopher, who was asked for an opinion and in turn called in Commander Minoru Genda, an experienced air group commander. Genda looked over the plan admiringly and said at once: "Difficult but possible."

Despite precautions, rumors of the Pearl Harbor plan spread quickly in official Tokyo. In January a Japanese diplomat, in his cups at a party at the Peruvian Embassy, boasted that "the American fleet will disappear." U.S. Ambassador Joseph C. Grew wrote in his diary on January 27:

> There is a lot of talk around town to the effect that the Japanese, in case of a break with the United States, are planning to go all out in a surprise mass attack at Pearl Harbor. Of course I informed our Government.

Washington passed the report to Admiral Husband E. Kimmel, the new commander at Pearl Harbor, with the comment: "Naval Intelligence places no credence in these rumors."

In April Ohnishi and Genda gave Yamamoto a general outline of what was now called Z Operation, isolating two major obstacles—the difficulty of launching torpedoes in the shallows of Pearl Harbor, and the necessity of achieving surprise. The scheme had about a 60 percent chance of success, Ohnishi thought. Fukudome was less optimistic; he rated the chances at 40 percent.

Yamamoto was not deterred by difficulties, and in May began training the fleet for a blow at Pearl Harbor. The most expert of the Navy's pilots were assembled to drill with bombs and torpedoes. Yamamoto chose Kagoshima Bay off southern Kyushu, where torpedo planes practiced for weeks, buzzing over the nearby city of Kagoshima and diving abruptly to within a few feet of the water in the harbor—an approach much like that to be made in Pearl Harbor. The planes whizzed past a long jetty, which had been chosen for its marked similarity to Battleship Row in the distant American base.

The practice went on until each pilot had made more than fifty runs at the target—and each day they practiced carrier landings at sea, beyond sight of the shore. They flew back to their base, skimming the wave tops. Kagoshima's civilians grew accustomed to the planes and their inexplicable maneuvers; the Navy Circus, they called it.

Not far away, bombing squadrons were at work, led by Commander Mitsuo Fuchida, dropping dummy bombs on an outline target of a battleship on a sandy islet. Farther out in the bay dive bombers droned up and down the sky, blasting targets. Less spectacularly, Minoru Genda and a few pilots and torpedo specialists experimented in nearby waters, working with wooden fins until they perfected shallow-draft torpedo runs. The pilots knew only that they were drilling for some special mission, perhaps in the event of a new war. Some key men, like Fuchida, got hints of the secret. Genda told Fuchida one day, "Don't be alarmed, but you have been chosen to lead the air force, in case we strike Pearl Harbor."

In April Fukudome astonished Rear Admiral Ryunosuke Kusaka, of the First Air Fleet staff, by handing him a secret document, a thick notebook filled with descriptive facts, statistics and spy reports on Pearl Harbor. Kusaka saw that it was complete but for one detail—there was no operations plan for the strike.

"That's what we want you to do," Fukudome said. Kusaka was at first overwhelmed by the difficulties, and when he went to the *Yamato* to confer with Yamamoto, he was still skeptical.

"It is appealing, but extremely risky," Kusaka said. "Worst of all, Admiral Nagumo does not like it."

Yamamoto smiled. "You are thinking that it's the dream of a gambler. You see me only as a mah-jongg and *shogi* player. There are other considerations." Yamamoto took Kusaka aside to upbraid him gently, speaking privately so that Kusaka would not lose face before the others: "Pearl Harbor is my idea and I need your support. We must push it through; it is our only hope in a war with America. I hope you will win over Nagumo—but please do not oppose me again. I am going to see this to the finish."

Kusaka did not forget Yamamoto's tact. "You must support a man who treats you like that," he told a friend. He began work on a detailed plan of attack, coordinating the carrier fleet, torpedo planes, dive bombers and high-level bombers.

Yamamoto drilled his men through late summer and into the autumn, determined to overcome objections in advance with proof that his crews could accomplish anything. By now the commander had moved his battle line to the mid-Pacific, through Hawaii, Midway and the Aleutian Islands.

In September, Yamamoto took his plan to Tokyo for several days of war games. There was little enthusiasm for the plan on the Naval General Staff, and the chief, Admiral Osami Nagano, would not give his personal approval. The conference moved boldly enough in other directions, deciding to strike simultaneously in Malaya, Burma, the Solomons and other Central Pacific islands, the Dutch Indies and the Philippines. It was only Hawaii that seemed too risky. Even if all went well at Pearl Harbor, the conference concluded, the attack would be costly, with the loss of two or three aircraft carriers. The real basis of opposition was the plan's unorthodoxy, "radically opposed to the well-established concepts of Japanese naval strategy." Nagano also warned that they must give Ambassadors Nomura and Kurusu time to complete negotiations in Washington.

Yamamoto went forward with his training as if the Navy

supported the plan unanimously. On October 9 he called hundreds of fleet officers to the *Yamato* in Hiroshima Bay and told them tersely that Japan faced war or strangulation, and warned them that the Navy must be ready for any emergency.

To Tamechi Hara, a young destroyer captain in the throng, the commander's manner was more menacing than his words. Hara wrote:

> Yamamoto's brief words were delivered in a low voice, yet they struck like a thunderbolt. Every officer was stunned. I felt frozen in my place.
>
> Admiral Yamamoto clamped his jaws as he stopped talking and looked around as if trying to look into the eyes of each individual. He looked more glum than stern as he walked slowly away from the podium.

Events moved rapidly as Japan prepared for war. Prince Konoye and his cabinet resigned and Hideki Tojo took over. Still Nagano had not given approval for the Pearl Harbor attack. One night when they were alone at *shogi*, Yamamoto startled Watanabe by slamming his fist on the table and saying angrily "I'll resign. Watanabe, he will approve, or fight his war without me." Watanabe merely smiled. "Go ahead," he said. Yamamoto grinned back at him. A few days later there was word from the Navy: proceed with plans for Z Operation.

Training became more hectic. There was now little more than a month to prepare for the kill of the American fleet. Yamamoto's assault crews were ready, and in early November he ordered Nagumo to prepare his task force to sail from the Inland Sea late in the month. His air of confidence gave no hint of the anxieties he revealed to an old friend.

Four days after he had ordered the task force to sail, he wrote of the coming war to his classmate Teikichi Hori, now a retired vice admiral:

> How miserable it is to have to say . . . that this is fate. But then further arguments pro and con will avail nothing.
>
> Now that we have reached the stage where "the Emperor alone must grieve over the state of affairs in the land," the only thing that can save the situation is the final Imperial decision. But how difficult that will be, in view of the present situation in the country!

What a strange position I find myself in now—having to make a decision diametrically opposed to my personal opinion, with no choice but to push full speed in pursuance of that decision. Is that, too, fate?

And what a bad start we've made . . .

The Imperial decision did not come. Emperor Hirohito seemed helpless. The Emperor listened without comment as Hideki Tojo told an Imperial conference on December 1 that British and American demands threatened Japan's prosperity and existence, that the most intensive diplomatic efforts had failed, and that the Army and Navy were ready for action. "Things have reached this point," Tojo said. "We have no recourse but to go to war against the United States, Great Britain and the Netherlands . . ."

The Emperor had left quietly, accepting the unanimous decision of his government.

By now Yamamoto's task force was well on its way to a secret rendezvous.

THE SHIPS DISAPPEARED ONE BY ONE, as if bound on separate routine missions—four large carriers, *Shokaku*, *Zuikaku*, *Akagi* and *Kaga*, and the light ones, *Hiryu* and *Soryu*, escorted by two battleships and three cruisers, nine destroyers, three submarines and eight oil tankers. The last of them came to the rendezvous in Tankan Bay in the bleak Kuriles on November 21, an anchorage surrounded by snow-covered hills and a few fishing huts. The men loaded thousands of oil drums aboard, in case rough weather prevented refueling at sea; they worked under strict security, with no refuse allowed to be thrown overboard, and garbage burned on the pier. No one had shore leave.

Behind them, the Inland Sea crackled with the normal heavy radio traffic of the fleet, and Yamamoto's staff added to the deception by detaining the regular wireless operators from the carriers, so that their distinctive touch would be recognized by enemy monitors.

Admiral Nagumo held a final conference aboard the *Akagi* on November 23, and the force sailed on the foggy dawn of November 26, plunging eastward into the teeth of a bitter wind.

The task force sailed through high seas and fog day after day. Each dawn found the oil tankers scattered by the rough seas, and the destroyers spent hours herding them back into place.

Aboard the carriers, where planes were lashed on deck, wing to wing, pilots spent many hours inspecting them and warming the engines; below, flight leaders pored over the plans of Pearl Harbor and Honolulu. Most of the men still known to few. The ships plowed on, into the empty seas lying between Midway and the Aleutians.

At last, on December 2, Yamamoto ended the suspense with a radio signal: "Climb Mount Niitaka"—which meant "Proceed with attack." The strike was on. The crews were told, and for several hours the ships howled with banzais and toasts. The next day, all pilots were drilled on the new assignments in concentrated briefings, studying targets at Pearl Harbor and the airfields and Ford Island. Kusaka had kept a large plaster model of Pearl Harbor locked in his stateroom, and now had it taken to the hangar deck of the *Akagi*, where it could be studied.

At dawn of December 6 Yamamoto's final message came in to the *Akagi*:

"The moment has arrived. The rise or fall of our country is at stake . . ."

All hands were called to stations, and as the historic "Z" flag that Togo had flown at Tsushima was run up, Yamamoto's message was shouted into the loudspeakers. The men cheered wildly, and several officers made impassioned speeches. The task force turned to the south. The next day, December 7, the first wave of planes took off at 6 A.M.—forty torpedo planes, fifty-one dive bombers and forty-nine of Fuchida's high-level bombers.

Just north of Oahu the 140 planes of the first wave flew over a white cloud bank. Fuchida and the big bombers were at 9000 feet when the Commander saw a break in the clouds and a strand of surf below. The harbor and the U.S. fleet, Honolulu and the sprawling bases and airfields all seemed peacefully asleep. A few minutes later Fuchida fired his signal pistol into the air to announce that surprise was complete.

At 7:49 he radioed the prearranged attack signal to his planes: "To . . . To . . . To . . . To." Four minutes later, when the torpedo planes were still making their runs on the battleships below and no bombs had fallen, Fuchida sent a premature message back to Nagumo, a coded signal that the attack had succeeded: "Tora . . . Tora . . . Tora . . ."*

The message was heard far to the north on the *Akagi*, where Nagumo and Kusaka, overcome with emotion, silently shook hands.

BY A FREAK SKIP SIGNAL, the low-powered transmission from Fuchida's bomber was also picked up on the waiting *Yamato*, three thousand miles away in the anchorage at Hiroshima. The tension in the operations room was broken by the young communications officer, who rushed in, bellowing, "The 'To' signal! The 'To' signal. The planes are striking." He handed the message to the staff duty officer who said in a wavering voice, "You have heard. The time of the dispatch was three-nineteen."

Fukudome looked at Yamamoto. The commander's mouth was clamped into a white-lipped line. He stared at the duty officer with a solemn, wide-eyed expression.

Ugaki turned to the communications officer, who was in the doorway. "Did you receive this directly from the plane?"

"Yes, sir. Directly."

"Remarkable," Ugaki said. "Remarkable."

The elated officer bowed and disappeared.

Soon messages from Nagumo were coming in continuously, confirming the *kishu-seiko*—the successful sneak attack; a cruiser had been hit . . . a battleship . . . thirty parked planes had been bombed and twenty-seven were burning. Yamamoto rarely changed his expression as the details came in.

An American message also came through, sent in plain text by an operator too excited to wait for coding. The *Yamato*'s communications officer read it: "Japanese are attacking. This is not a drill. Japanese attack. This is for real." The officers roared with laughter. Fukudome saw a fleeting smile on Yamamoto's face.

By 1 P.M., Pearl Harbor time, Fuchida landed on the

---

* The Japanese message was "Tiger . . . tiger . . . tiger," the coded signal saying that surprise was complete. The words were inspired by a Japanese proverb, "A tiger goes out two thousand miles and returns without fail."

Akagi, anxious to rearm and refuel for another strike; planes were already lined up for the takeoff. The Commander went to the bridge and found himself in the midst of a heated argument. Nagumo had forbidden another blow at Pearl Harbor, and remained adamant despite Fuchida's pleas. "Anticipated results have been achieved," Nagumo said firmly. Fuchida and others argued in vain that good targets remained, that the American defense was pathetic and that, best of all, another blow might lure the carriers within range.

At 1:30 P.M. the *Akagi* swung about for the return to Japan and signaled the task force to follow.

Aboard the *Yamato*, Yamamoto seemed to divine the distant move with a sixth sense.

"It would be wonderful," a senior officer said, "if Nagumo attacks once more—wipes out the base."

Yamamoto's eyes flashed angrily, and he spoke in a barely audible voice, as if to himself, "Nagumo will soon return."

A few minutes later a report from the task force bore him out.

Fukudome went onto the deck in the dawn. "I breathed deeply of the fresh morning air. What a calm morning it is—though our great war has begun today. How serene it is, and how serene is our commander."

The next day, Watanabe and Yamamoto were alone, playing *shogi*, when they were interrupted to hear a shortwave radio broadcast from America. They heard the slow, full voice of Franklin Roosevelt addressing the Congress, asking for a declaration of war and speaking bitterly of a "day that will live in infamy."

The American people, an announcer said, were united as never before; the nation was seething with anger and clamoring for revenge.

Yamamoto listened intently, smiling slightly, but as the broadcast ended he had a somber look: "That's too bad. Too bad. Watanabe, I don't know whether you or I will die first, but if I should die before you, tell the Emperor that the Navy did not plan it this way from the beginning . . ."

3

The Hunters

AMONG THE MILLIONS OF AMERICANS who were caught up in Pearl Harbor Day were five young pilots of the U.S. Air Corps, hardly more than boys. None of them had ever heard of Isoroku Yamamoto. Within sixteen months they were to lead the remarkable mission that cost the Japanese admiral his life.

They were obscure members of the huge air force now belatedly expanding to meet the Axis threat: Besby Frank Holmes of San Francisco; John W. Mitchell of Enid, Mississippi; Rex Barber of Culver, Oregon; Douglas Canning of Wayne, Nebraska; and Tom Lanphier of Detroit.

Four of these pilots were recent graduates of the flying schools and had no more than three or four hours in fighter planes. The youngest of them was twenty-two, the oldest, twenty-six.

SECOND LIEUTENANT BESBY FRANK HOLMES, who was wearing a new brown pin-stripe suit, was among the small congregation at Mass when the planes came in over Pearl Harbor. First there were only the chimes of the sanctus bells and the singsong voice of the priest in the Army chapel, then the shuddering blasts of the bombs, from some miles away. The service went on for a few minutes and ended abruptly, but people were slow to leave. No one knew what was happening.

Holmes went to his room in the Air Corps barracks. The radio was blaring, and his roommate turned on him: "Japs attacking! We've got war! Don't panic! The Army has it under control." His voice was unnaturally shrill.

They ran into the street, commandeered a civilian's car, and drove rapidly to Wheeler Field. They flashed past Pearl Harbor as the *Arizona* exploded and rolled over.

Holmes's hangar was a mass of flaming wreckage, still roaring at one end and stinking of gasoline and burned rubber. Fifty of the sixty planes were gone. Holmes drove to the gunnery range beyond, where the P-36's of another squadron were parked, low-winged fighters already obsolete. A line chief handed him a parachute pack and a .45 pistol and ran with him toward a waiting fighter. When they were in the open, crossing the strip, a Japanese plane swept down, strafing. Holmes fell and emptied his pistol at the enemy fighter. "You got him," someone yelled. "You broke his shield." The plane flew away and Holmes rose, dusting off his new suit, threw away his pistol and climbed into the P-36.

He fired five of the six starter cartridges, but the engine failed to start. The chief came out and started her on the first try. As the chief began crawling out, Holmes pushed him back into the cockpit. The chief looked frightened. "Hell, no," he said, "I ain't taking her up. My ass stays down here."

"No, no," Holmes said. "Just arm the guns—I'm going up."

He was in the air within half an hour after leaving Mass, but the enemy had gone. The only shots fired came up at him from anti-aircraft batteries around the fields, when he had left the range strip. Two other pilots had shot down enemy planes that morning, but Holmes found only an empty sky. It was his second flight in a P-36, and he had never fired a gun in the air. Two days earlier he had passed his twenty-fourth birthday.

Besby Holmes was a black-haired boy of one hundred and thirty pounds, fresh from flight training at Hawaii's Luke Field. Back home in San Francisco he had been a state chess champion and a junior college swimmer and a boxer. Barely ten months before, in March, 1941, he had joined the Air Corps.

He could remember the day, in 1933, when he first knew that he would become a pilot. He had been fishing from a pier in San Francisco Bay on a bright, airy summer morning, when a flight of new P-36's winged low overhead in formation, swift and awesome, fighters of a kind he had never seen. He thought: I've got to fly one of those some day.

He had been sworn as a cadet in a San Francisco recruiting station with a group of twenty-five, all strangers, one of them Tom Lanphier, whom he was to meet much later, on Guadalcanal. Holmes had volunteered for overseas duty to get into fighters, and last summer reached Hawaii, completed training and was now a green recruit for the 47th Fighter Squadron. He had thought that war must be very near. The squadron had been on twenty-four-hour alert, under tight security, flying patrols every day, until yesterday, December 6, the alert had been canceled, and the men of the 47th had relaxed.

THE FIRST SUNDAY OF DECEMBER had been unseasonably warm in Charlotte, North Carolina. In the late afternoon a crowd of moviegoers streamed from the Carolina Theater, still caught up in the drama of the World War hero, Sergeant Alvin York, as played by Gary Cooper. Newsboys assailed them on the sidewalk, gobbling the news:

"Japs Strike Pearl Harbor!"
"Pacific Fleet Wiped Out!"

Among the crowd was a short, slight young man with an airman's cap on the back of his head, wearing the new bars of a first lieutenant. He bought a copy of the Charlotte *News* and moved away at a halting pace, reading as he went. He was John W. Mitchell, twenty-six, operations officer and most experienced pilot of the 70th Fighter Squadron of the infant U.S. Army Air Corps, stranded here by the breakdown of a P-40 during the recent maneuvers in the Carolinas. He spent the next few hours trying to reach his commanding officer, Captain Henry Viccellio, in California; it was very late when the call went through.

"Vic, what the hell do you want me to do? Come on back?"

"No, stay there until you get that plane ready, then fly in. We're due to ship out January eight, but God knows what'll happen now. This place is a revolving madhouse."

"Well, I'm gonna get married next week."

"Too late for that," Viccellio said. No more easy deferments."

Mitchell laughed. "We won't hold you up. I'll stop in Texas on the way out."

"Well, remember us if you can. I need you, Mitch. My God, when I think about getting these green kids ready for war . . . don't let anything happen to that damned plane. They're already beginning to cry for 'em—and condolences to the bride."

John Mitchell was a stray Mississippian. In his brief career he had been valedictorian of his high school class in Enid, Mississippi, a scholarship winner, economics major, batamweight boxer and student waiter at Columbia University, a veteran of a three-year hitch in the Army as a coast artilleryman in Hawaii, a tournament tennis player, a sports writer and liquor store clerk. He was an easygoing leader who had quickly won over the young pilots of the squadron, but was unsparing of himself and restless at inaction.

His pilots already told barracks tales of Mitchell's recent tour as an observer in England, where he had borrowed a Spitfire, sneaked across the Channel, and was said—erroneously—to have shot down a German fighter.

In November, 1941, Mitchell went into the large-scale southern maneuvers, flying fighter missions in his P-40 off a grass strip in a small South Carolina town, drilling the squadron from dawn to dark and helping Henry Viccellio mold it into a fighting unit.

Mitchell had been an outdoorsman since childhood in the hills of northern Mississippi, when as a self-reliant twelve-year-old he had often stayed alone in the woods, living off the country by fishing and shooting small game. In those years he had acquired an almost infallible sense of direction, from long practice in finding his way by the sun and stars, practice that later made navigation in the air easier for him.

Mitchell became a flying cadet in 1939, just as the Air Corps began to feel the pressures of war, and by July, 1940, he had graduated from Randolph and Kelly fields and joined a fighter squadron. He soon met Henry Viccellio, who had completed his training only a year earlier. Viccellio was a popular commander and an Air Corps veteran who knew the ropes—he had enlisted as a private in 1934.

Even after the Carolina maneuvers Mitchell knew that the pilots of the squadron were not ready for war. By comparison with the veterans of the Royal Air Force, they were mere beginners.

Even this partially trained squadron was soon to be snatched away. Mitchell flew west alone in his P-40 during the second week of December, 1941, stopped for two days in Dallas for his wedding, and reported back to Hamilton Field near San Francisco.

He found that the "veteran" 70th Squadron had been stripped of its most experienced men by an Air Corps desperately rushing men and planes into the Pacific. Pilots, crew chiefs, mechanics, armorers and all the rest had been shipped out to Java by way of Australia. These men were to die, almost to the man, when the Japanese sank the old converted collier, *Langley*, still in use as an aircraft carrier.

Captain Viccellio wheedled a few experienced replacements from the Air Corps, but for the rest, he had green graduates of flying schools, promising youngsters like Tom Lanphier, Rex Barber and Douglas Canning. To Mitchell and Viccellio, these were only names, as they began the task of rebuilding the dismembered 70th.

HEADQUARTERS SQUADRON of the 35th Fighter Group was two days out of San Francisco on the *President Garfield* on December 7, bound for some island outpost, its P-39 Airacobra fighters snug in the hold and the pilots in their bunks, sleeping off a spree. The soberer ones were awake first, crowding about the radios, hearing the faint crackling voices of alarm as announcers in California gave hurried and confused reports of the attack on Hawaii.

Second Lieutenant Rex Barber was one of the last pilots to be shaken awake; the news sobered him. Barber's first thought was of his uncle Edgar King, at home in Culver, Oregon, who had trained as a fighter pilot during the World War. Since boyhood Rex had been dazzled—ruined, his mother said—by the old man's hair-raising tales of flying and dogfights and alluring women who roamed the world in chase of pursuit pilots. Rex could picture Uncle Edgar and his parents, hearing the war news at home; his mother would be fighting back tears, but Edgar would be giddy with delight. "He's going to be an ace!" he would say. "You mark my word. I always knew he would."

Barber was almost twenty-five years old, and a veteran of only four hours' flying in a P-40, but already he was known as a fearless, reckless pilot. He was loud, bull-necked and strong, a former baseball and basketball star in school and college; he had ridden horseback and hunted most of his life, near the village which had been laid out and founded by his father.

In 1940, when war seemed very near, Rex had enlisted in the Army and was accepted as an air cadet. His first triumph in uniform was on the firing range at Fort Lewis, in Tacoma, where he qualified as expert with pistol, rifle and machine gun—and when a skeptical officer forced him to repeat the tests, shot even higher scores.

Rex was one of four in a class of more than one hundred chosen as fighter pilots; and had joined Headquarters Squadron of the 70th. Since he had never flown a fighter, he was hurried to Hamilton Field with several other men, given four hours of air time in a P-40 and returned as a fighter pilot, theoretically qualified for overseas duty.

The fliers had smuggled their own liquor aboard the *Garfield* and their howling two-day celebration afloat was accompanied by phonograph music and the din of interminable card and dice games.

Most of the whiskey was gone by December 7, and few of the pilots wanted to drink. The day seemed to stretch on forever. The big white liner slowed and wallowed as the captain awaited orders from the States. A sitting duck, the fliers thought, lying there in her gleaming white with a blue band about her stack; they felt very much alone in the Pacific, which they imagined to be swarming with enemy ships and submarines. They went to bed early, but were jarred awake soon afterward by the furious pounding of the engines, as the captain turned back to California under forced draft. They made it home in one day.

A SQUADRON OF B-17's had come from the east on December 6, using Hamilton Field as a stopover on their way to Hawaii. The bombers were enormous in the eyes of the fighter pilots who hung around to watch them being readied for the Pacific flight. The line crews worked for half a day, removing excess weight to increase the fuel capacity.

Second Lieutenant Douglas Canning, of the 70th Squadron, who was standing emergency guard duty at a gate, watched the guns taken from the bombers and saw the B-17's waddle onto the runway and take off, circling until the flight pattern was complete. They flew westward unarmed, bound for Hawaii.

Later in the day Canning was relieved at the gate and sent to a crew filling sandbags and building revetments for planes; more than once the walls of piled bags toppled over, and the inexperienced men struggled to rebuild them, working until late in the night, in the glare of lights. Canning, like most of his mates, had never been in a fighter plane, though he was three months out of Kelly Field.

He was asleep when news of Pearl Harbor came, was aroused by shouts of others in the hotel, and at first thought they were celebrating. He got up and went back to the sandbag crew.

Doug Canning was a baby-faced boy of twenty-two, but he was a graduate of Wayne State Teachers College in Nebraska. He had first flown at the age of eight, in an antique Curtiss Robin piloted by an uncle, Guy Strickland, who had been a sergeant in the World War.

Canning, the son of a bank teller, was an apt student in school, and a prospective teacher until he took a civilian pilot training course in college and joined the Air Corps. He had gone to Hamilton Field in September, 1941, to check out in P-36 fighters and sail for the Central Pacific.

There was only one P-36 at Hamilton, and after most of his squadron had taken brief flights, the old plane broke down with a cracked cylinder. Canning and five others were unable to check out.

In early January, as Hamilton Field began to recover from the shock of the Japanese attacks, the inexperienced boys of the squadron were given final training before embarkation. Two aging lieutenants lectured them for an hour and sent them to the flight line to get into late-model fighters that had just arrived, the new P-40-E's.

They took off gingerly in the new ships, since the field teemed with work crews hurrying to expand the field for an influx of men and planes. As Canning came in to land, the control tower was barking instructions so rapidly that he became rattled, and he veered to the left of the runway, knocking down and scattering a bevy of WPA workmen. Another of the pilots, Jack Jacobson, also had troubles. The fighter's long nose blocked his vision so that he could not set up the easy glide path he had learned in trainers, and only after many unnerving passes did he nurse the ship to a bumpy landing. "I thought they were going to have to shoot me down," he said.

The final drill in their combat qualification was air-to-ground gunnery, which they practiced at sea. An instructor dropped a glass ball packed with aluminum powder, which left a slick on the surface and provided a target for the young gunners. In these last days Canning flew without mishap, and became renowned in the squadron for his remarkable vision; he could see like an eagle. Their skipper, Captain Viccellio, called Rex Barber "Cateyes," but it was usually Canning who first spotted distant objects.

COLONEL THOMAS G. LANPHIER, SR., heard the news by radio in his San Francisco hotel room, and before the announcer finished the first meager account, telephoned his son Tom in a nearby hotel. Tom responded sleepily after half a dozen rings, and after his first shock, realized that he was not so surprised as he might have been; his father had persuaded him to enter the Air Corps months before, arguing that the United States would enter the war sooner or later, and that pilots would fare better than infantrymen.

Colonel Lanphier was an old-timer from another era of American aviation, a West Pointer who had trained at Issoudun in France during the World War, had flown on pioneering flights to Alaska and Brazil, had commanded old Dehavilland bomber squadrons, and the First (and only) Pursuit Squadron. He was now on duty as an air intelligence officer on General George C. Marshall's staff in Washington. This week he had come to say goodbye to his son before he sailed for a Pacific base, a second-generation fighter pilot.

When the broadcast was over, Lanphier dressed and went out, looking for news, but could hear only wild rumors from Hawaii, even from his friends in newspaper offices. There was a rash of local news. San Francisco was near panic. A state of emergency had been declared and guards were posted everywhere; shipping in the harbor was halted, and all service leaves had been canceled. In the confusion traffic was blocked on the Golden Gate Bridge and a state guard had shot a woman motorist; eager sabateur hunters had fired on a crew of painters beneath the bridge.

Policemen and national guardsmen had surrounded the Japanese districts and arrests had begun. Plainclothesmen dragged a man from the Aki Hotel on Post Street while a Japanese Salvation Army band played "Marching Through Georgia." Windows of Japanese shops were smashed, and one store window bore a crude sign: "Jap-hunting licenses here."

Lanphier returned to Hamilton Field, where he was assigned as officer of the day on a small part of the base, duty that was to occupy him for many days to come. The rest passed in a blur of card games in BOQ, or sitting on the flight line to watch men of the squadron in their few planes at practice, gliding down, touching and roaring off again.

Lanphier was barely twenty-six years old, but it had been twelve years since he had soloed his first plane, an elderly Army Jenny that he had wheeled proudly over Detroit. Two of his father's second lieutenants of the First Pursuit Group had taught the boy secretly, and after seven or eight hours at dual controls, they had sent him aloft. He was fourteen. Tom's dream of a lifetime in the air was shattered that night when the outraged Colonel discovered the clandestine flight; the old man had whaled him without mercy and confined Lieutenants Woodring and Cornelius to the post for months.

Young Lanphier went to high school in Detroit and entered journalism school at Stanford in 1933, but when his father suffered financial losses, was forced to alternate between college and odd jobs—grocery clerk, ranch hand and newspaperman—for several years. He had worked on the San Francisco *News*, reviewing books and plays and covering a labor beat on the docks.

Lanphier learned to fly for the second time in the civilian pilot training program at Palo Alto, and in November graduated as an Air Corps cadet and was sent to the 70th Fighter Squadron at Hamilton Field.

Lanphier was one of the most talented of Viccellio's pilots, fearless and able; he took off in his first P-40 like a combat veteran, and the Captain knew that he need not nurse this one. Lanphier was lean, wiry and strong, and the most articulate of the 70th's garrulous crew. His mates found him somewhat aloof, with interests they did not share, and though he was popular, they found his speech noticeably precise and his omnivorous reading remarkable. He played poker well and was the keynoter of many bull sessions, holding forth on random topics with easy assurance, a dark, curly-haired spell-binder—a supersalesman, as many pilots remembered him.

AT LAST, ON JANUARY 20, 1942, the 70th Fighter Squadron sailed for the Fiji Islands aboard the *President Monroe*, 44 officers and 219 enlisted men, one of the green-est of Air Corps units moving off to war in these hectic days. Just before departure, Captain Viccellio got a glimpse of the dark future, as seen from Washington, when a friend came to San Francisco from the east. Someone at Air Corps head-quarters had asked how the 70th Squadron was to be sup-plied on Fiji, and a staff officer had replied: "Don't give it a thought; it won't be there long enough to worry about it." The Japanese were expected to invade the Fijis and many other Pacific islands.

The ship had been stocked for civilians, and the men dined off such delicacies as squab and Baked Alaska. Waiters in tailcoats served the meals. The men made a pretext of taking calisthenics and listened half-heartedly to lectures and stood torpedo watches, but Viccellio had given them their cue as they left San Francisco: "You'd better live it up while you can, because when you step off this ship, you're gonna meet hard times. And they're gonna last. And last."

They were sixteen days at sea, sailing in a three-ship convoy of transports, huddling together until they were half-way between New Zealand and the Fijis, when their two companions turned for Australia. The voyage passed swiftly. As Doug Canning remembered it. "We left a trail of hooch bottles all the way from the Golden Gate to Suva Harbor."

4

After Victory

THE NAVY CAME TO PAY HOMAGE TO YAMAMOTO, and for weeks the fleet anchorage wore a festive air as officers and Tokyo politicians shuttled across the bay in the yellow launches to board the *Yamato*.

The Emperor had been among the first to send greetings:

> At the very outbreak of this war our Combined Fleet has displayed a brilliant strategy and fought bravely. At Hawaii it has heavily crushed the enemy's fleet and air strength . . . we extend our deepest praise to our fighting forces, officers and men alike. If they strive harder we foresee a magnificent future for our Empire.

The Emperor had also sent a handsome set of sake cups, from which the visitors drank victory toasts.

Ceremonial display aboard the *Yamato* was the marvel of civilians and the envy of naval visitors. Guests who came to lunch while the giant ship was in port saw Yamamoto in his splendor.

At 11:50 A.M. a Navy band assembled; five minutes later the staff, in starched and gleaming whites, gathered at their long table in the dining room; and promptly at noon the chief steward, Petty Officer Heijiro Omi, rapped smartly on the Admiral's door. The band blasted away at a stirring march as the *Gensui* strode out and paced down a corridor to join his staff officers, who waited with bowed heads. The band played light popular tunes for half an hour during luncheon; the food was usually Western style.

Young officers from headquarters snickered privately and observed that since Pearl Harbor every man in Yamamoto's entourage had acquired new dignity and assumed superior airs. "The Victory disease," the Tokyo gossips said, was epidemic on the *Yamato*, but all were carefully respectful to Yamamoto, whose prestige was now unrivaled in Japan.

Admiral Yonai gave a sumptuous party ashore in Yamamoto's honor, attended by flag officers and the most influential men from Tokyo. There was heady news from every theater. The *Prince of Wales* and the *Repulse* were sunk with incredible ease on the third day of war; the U.S. carrier *Saratoga* was torpedoed and badly damaged; Singapore fell on February 5, and by mid-March the occupation of Java and Sumatra was almost complete. The Japanese people were delirious with joy, as if the war had been won. Newspapers told of a distressed and defeated America, its ghostly cities subjected to blackouts, unwilling women dragged to work in war plants like convict laborers, and a frightened public now turning to leaders like Father James E. Coughlin, the Fascist priest.

Yamamoto was unmoved by the public frenzy. Less than two weeks after Pearl Harbor he had written his elderly sister, Mrs. Kazuko Takahashi, in Nagaoka:

> . . . Finally our war has begun. I feel that it may last for several decades. There's no use in our being impatient. Back home I hear that people are making empty boasts—if we listened to them then there could be no good education, no increased production. The more serious our national emergency, the more all should do their duty.
>
> The sinking of four or five warships is no cause for wild celebration. There will be times of defeat as well as victory . . .

The geisha, Chioko Kawai, ill with pneumonia, came down from Tokyo to be near Yamamoto, and they often spent the evenings in her apartment ashore. He was deeply concerned, and his doctor made frequent calls on her; she improved slowly. She sometimes played the *samisen* and sang for him, but his visits were brief. The commander's time was increasingly taken up by the pressures of war, and Chioko soon returned to Tokyo.

By mid-January a strange new mood pervaded the *Yamato*. Victory had left a vacuum, and no one seemed to know what should be done next. There was no detailed plan for fighting the war to a finish. Admiral Fukudome noted a change in Yamamoto: "As he went about his duties of daily life he wore an air of concern . . . He was restless."

Yamamoto fumed because the government did not press a diplomatic offensive, looking toward negotiations for peace. He and Fukudome held long, melancholy conferences. Fukudome remembered these days for the "feeling of emptiness" which persisted in the wake of such dazzling conquests.

"It is not so hard to open a war as to conclude it, Shigeru," Yamamoto once told Fukudome. "We must find a way to capitalize on our victories; the government should work with us in a combined strategy, but that will never be. How can we now negotiate? There is no country to mediate for us. We must push our destiny to the limit, while there is yet time."

Discussions in the operations room grew more heated. Yamamoto and Fukudome and many flag officers who came aboard were insistent that the first goals of conquest had been too modest. They must strike again—but there was still the threat of the American carriers.

In mid-January Yamamoto sent Ugaki and Kuroshima to work, and they disappeared for four days, visited only by stewards who took them tea and rice. The chief of staff emerged with a plan for a blow at Midway or Hawaii that would lure the American carrier fleet to its doom; Kuroshima produced an elaborate scheme calling for sixteen task forces to strike at Midway and the Aleutians. Yamamoto joined the staff sessions that followed as the plan was simplified, and was soon fighting for the plan in Tokyo.

Headquarters resisted as it had the Pearl Harbor plan, urging instead operations against Australia, but Yamamoto refused to give up the Midway plan. On April 18 Tokyo was shocked into submission, when Jimmy Doolittle's bomber pilots, flying from Rear Admiral Marc Mitscher's carrier *Hornet*, bombed the Japanese capital.

Yamamoto got word of the carriers from the fishing vessel *Nitto Maru* at 6:30 A.M. and ordered Vice Admiral Nobutake Kondo to sea to cut off the U.S. ships; he also sent out planes of the 21st Air Flotilla from Tokyo. It was too late. Kondo had barely cleared the harbor when word came to the *Yamato* that Tokyo had been bombed. Official Tokyo reacted almost hysterically.

Yamamoto studied incoming messages with growing surprise. American planes had dropped bombs on Yokohama, Nagoya and other cities, and all had escaped unscathed. There could be no carrier planes of such range. Yamamoto was even more baffled when he had positive identification of Doolittle's B-25's, for he could not believe that heavy bombers could take off from carriers.

The strike depressed Yamamoto; he took to his cabin for an entire day, refusing to see callers. By the next day, more insistent messages went from the *Yamato* to Tokyo, where opposition to the Midway plan was weakened. The Midway attack seemed a logical response to this raid. Yamamoto ordered the fleet to prepare for the offensive.

On May 27 a striking force of nineteen ships, including four carriers, left Hiroshima Bay. And this was only the advance. Across the Pacific a fleet of 190 ships was converging on Midway and the Aleutians, the largest armada ever assembled for battle.

Yamamoto had made his farewells to his family: "Do not look upon me as your father any longer, for I have given my body and soul to the country. It will be my supreme glory to die for Japan."

He wrote to Chioko on the day the main force of carriers went to sea, using the fine brushes and the special paper he reserved for her letters. He dreamed of the day, he wrote, that they could go away together and be alone, leaving the world behind, but now he must take the fleet against the enemy. He did not look forward to the days ahead: "I imagine that very delightful moments may be few."

Yamamoto himself left with the main force on May 29, the *Yamato* leading six other battleships and an escort carrier, with a screen of destroyers and cruisers—thirty-four ships in all. Operations was supremely confident. Surprise would be complete and the Americans could at best send only two carriers against Japan's eight, since the *Lexington* had been reported sunk and the *Yorktown* sunk or badly damaged in the recent battle of the Coral Sea, which had been fought on May 8, the first battle ever fought between fleets lying more than a gunshot apart. Soon after, on May 15, two U.S. carriers had been seen in the Solomons, far to the south. The way was clear.

AT PEARL HARBOR the code-crackers of Hypo, who had been reading heavy Japanese traffic about the attack for weeks, had fully charted the approaching Japanese and identified even the ships and captains. For a few days skepticism by the Navy and Air Corps had frustrated Combat Intelligence. The code-crackers could read no more than 15 percent of Japanese messages with absolute accuracy; the rest was pieced out with bits of intelligence from past messages, or with the aid of other intelligence stations also monitoring the traffic. The most puzzling bits of code, as usual, were place names—in particular "AF," which was obviously Yamamoto's target.

Hypo argued that AF meant Midway, but others thought that AF was Hawaii, and that the islands should not be left unguarded in any case. It was Commander E. T. Layton who persuaded Admiral Nimitz that the code-crackers were right. When Washington remained unconvinced, Layton got permission from Nimitz to trap the enemy: a fake message was sent from Midway, reporting that the island's water filtration plant had broken down. Two days afterward Hypo had its proof, a Japanese dispatch asserting that AF was running out of water. It was enough for Nimitz. He prepared to ambush the Japanese carriers at Midway.

Nimitz called Admiral Halsey and his carriers, *Enterprise* and *Hornet*, from the South Pacific; squadrons of Flying Fortresses and PBY's flew out from California to bases on Hawaii and Midway. When Halsey's Task Force 16 arrived, Halsey was ill with a skin disease, and was put into a hospital; Admiral Raymond Spruance took over his task force.

On May 27, the day Admiral Nagumo took Yamamoto's main carrier force to sea, Admiral Jack Fletcher arrived at Pearl Harbor with Task Force 17 and one more carrier, the crippled *Yorktown*, whose case seemed hopeless, she should spend two or three months in drydock for repairs. Nimitz told his stunned engineers and repairmen that he must have her back within three days, and three days later, after 1400 men had worked around the clock, often in 120 degree heat, the *Yorktown* was ready. She sailed on May 30 and soon caught up with the fleet.

ON HIS FLAGSHIP, hundreds of miles to the west of Nagumo's striking force, Yamamoto was becoming slightly uneasy. He suffered an attack of diarrhea the day after he put to sea, and for several days ate only rice porridge. On May 31 he got the unsettling news of sudden activity in U.S. radio calls from Hawaii and the Aleutians, almost half of these messages classed as "urgent." Perhaps Nimitz was sending a task force toward Midway.

Yamamoto showed the messages to Captain Kameto Kuroshima of his staff. "These must be sent to Nagumo immediately."

Kuroshima protested. "He must have picked them up—and we can't risk breaking radio silence."

Yamamoto disagreed, but Kuroshima was determined that radio silence should not be broken, and withheld the messages on his own initiative. Nagumo's carrier fleet steamed eastward, ignorant of these signs of American watchfulness.

Far ahead of Yamamoto and the Main Force, Nagumo's fleet was shrouded in fog until June 3, when a patrol plane from Midway spotted the twenty-seven transports.

Before dawn on June 4, Nagumo began launching planes from his four carriers—*Akagi, Kaga, Hiryu* and *Soryu*—to strike at Midway. About an hour later an American patrol plane found Nagumo's carriers, and the battle was on. The striking force beat off eight American attacks during the next three hours—torpoedo planes, B-26's, Flying Fortresses, dive and glide bombers were all turned back, and many of the planes shot into the water. No Japanese ship had been yet hit.

It was only at 8:20 A.M., when he was debating whether to launch his second wave of planes, that Nagumo at last learned important news from a patrol plane: an American carrier had been sighted.

The *Yamato*'s radio room was monitoring the calls of Nagumo's search planes, and Yamamoto learned immediately that planes from Midway were attacking.

The mood was brighter on the commander's bridge this morning. Yamamoto had recovered from his stomach upset, ate his customary breakfast of rice, soup, eggs and fish. He and Ugaki wore whites and gloves, surrounded by the staff in blues or fatigues. The staff officers were ecstatic when they heard that an American carrier had been seen. The ruse was working; Nimitz had sent a lone carrier out to destruction. Captain Watanabe thought: It all turned out just as we wanted.

IN LESS THAN THIRTY MINUTES after he learned that a U.S. carrier was within range, Nagumo was struck by the first attack from Fletcher's fleet planes. Torpedo Squadron 8 from Mitscher's *Hornet* bored in, bravely but amateurishly, bunched together on the same approach, all fifteen planes shot down by Nagumo's Zeroes and gunners; only one man survived. It was now up to the dive bombers of *Enterprise* and *Yorktown.* They attacked just as Nagumo was launching planes. Incredibly, they struck three carriers within six minutes and left them mortally wounded, racked by fires and explosions: *Kaga, Akagi* and *Soryu* were doomed.

This news reached the *Yamato* almost immediately, Watanabe heard a message over the tube from the radio room: "The *Akagi* is on fire." The Admiral turned calmly to Kuroshima: "Shouldn't we confirm whether Nagumo has launched his torpedo strike?"

"There's no need for that, sir," Kuroshima said. "He must have attacked. It is part of the plan."

The radio room was now picking up a series of messages. The *Kaga* and *Sorya* were also burning. A real battle was raging, but the *Yamato* staff had no reason to assume that the damage was fatal. At 10:50 Yamamoto had a message from Rear Admiral Hiroaki Abe, second in command of the carrier force, who had taken over while Nagumo shifted his flag from the sinking *Akagi:*

> Fires are raging aboard the *Kaga, Soryu* and *Akagi* . . . We plan to have the *Hiryu* engage the enemy carriers. In the meantime, we are temporarily retiring to the north . . .

Yamamoto handed the sheet back to Ugaki. One sailor who watched him closely, Yeoman Noda, saw that the *Gensui's* face was "frozen," and another sailor remembered: "The Admiral and his staff looked at one another, their mouths tight shut. There was indescribable emptiness, cheerlessness and chagrin." As Yamamoto hurried toward the scene of the battle, he received more bad news: *Hiryu,* the last carrier of the striking force, had been sunk.

Yamamoto sat heavily in a chair on the bridge and did not stir for several moments, lost in thought, staring across the sea. Almost two hours passed before he sent a general order to the fleet, a victory message designed to bolster moral: the U.S. fleet practically destroyed, was retiring eastward. Combined Fleets units were "preparing to pursue the remnants" and were under orders to "immediately contact and destroy the enemy."

Near midnight, still worrying over plans for his forces now drawing together near Midway, Yamamoto's temper wore thin; he feared that Admiral Kondo's big force of destroyers, cruisers and battleships would be found by the U.S. carriers after dawn. His staff chattered away, offering suggestions, most of them absurd. One of the younger officers burst out, "But how can we apologize to His Majesty for this defeat?"

Yamamoto snapped, "Leave that to me. I am the only one who must apologize to His Majesty."

On June 6 Yamamoto learned that a submarine had sunk *Yorktown,* but he took little solace from the belated triumph. A few hours later he went to bed, refusing food. He reappeared two days later, when Nagumo's chief of staff, Admiral Ryunosuke Kusaka, came aboard to report on the disaster. The fat little officer still wore his oil-stained uniform, and limped from his wounds. There was a sad, quiet scene on the bridge before the staff, where Yamamoto thanked Kusaka for all he had done, and ordered that the survivors of the fleet be cared for. The two men then went into the commander's cabin alone, and Kusaka pleaded with Yamamoto to reorganize the carrier fleet and give them another chance at the enemy. "I understand." Yamamoto said hoarsely. His eyes were filled with tears.

When it became clear that the U.S. fleet could not be lured westward into a new battle, Yamamoto turned homeward. Censorship about the Midway disaster was so complete that returning crews were not given shore leave; others were penned in camps, closely guarded. Even the wounded Commander Mitsuo Fuchida, who had led the Pearl Harbor bombers, was taken to a hospital ashore and smuggled in at night on a covered stretcher by a back door.

IN THE WEEKS AFTER MIDWAY Yamamoto turned his attention to the south, where his forces had seized positions along the island chain shielding Australia. In May, during the battle of the Coral Sea, a small party of naval troops went ashore on Guadalcanal, with only two old field guns and three machine guns. It was the southernmost point of Japanese conquest, only 1200 miles from Australia.

After Midway, Yamamoto sent a battalion to Guadalcanal to build an airstrip near the coast; the troops hacked at the jungle with hand labor, slowly creating a runway of coral in the muck of the coastal plain. Within a few days, American intelligence passed word of this to Admiral Nimitz, who reacted vigorously. On August 7 the First U.S. Marine Division went ashore in the first American offensive of the war against Japan.

Yamamoto moved his base to Truk, a well-developed naval outpost near the new battle theater, and took over direction of the effort to drive the Americans from the Solomons, a conflict that was to rage for five months.

In October, convinced that this struggle would go on as long as Yamamoto had the strength to continue, Nimitz sent his most aggressive admiral, Bill Halsey, to command in the South Pacific, with his headquarters on New Caledonia.

The stage was set for Yamamoto's final campaign, and the men who were to hunt him to his death had already begun to gather on Guadalcanal.

In late August, soon after he arrived at Truk and moved his flag to the battleship *Musashi*, Yamamoto revealed his uneasiness to a friend: "I fear that I have perhaps one hundred days left to me, and I must complete my life in their passage."

The fleet got no hint of his state of mind. Each submarine that passed out of the harbor for sea duty moved close by the *Musashi*, its crew freshly changed from fatigues to dress uniforms, standing at attention to be reviewed by the Commander in Chief. Yamamoto did not disappoint them.

Goro Takase of his staff often saw him on the bridge or main deck, saluting the submarines, waving his hat in his right hand, and following them with his binoculars until they passed from sight. Takase was moved: "His concern for his subordinates struck to the heart of every sailor—the last of them must have been ready to die for him. His leadership reached to the very lowest reaches of the Navy and inspired us. His forces never wavered so long as he was in command."

THE LAST JAPANESE SOLDIER was evacuated from Guadalcanal on February 7, 1943, six months from the day the First Marine Division had gone ashore. In nearby waters lay the wrecks of both navies—135,000 tons of them Japanese and 126,000 Allied, chiefly American, a far greater toll than the battle of Jutland. In almost every meeting the Japanese had outmaneuvered the U.S. Pacific Fleet and followed to the letter Yamamoto's instructions—to destroy American capital ships.

Despite all, Yamamoto realized that he had lost once more. He had failed to relieve Guadalcanal. The Americans would quickly replace their losses; his own would never be made good. Japan had suffered its first land defeat of the war.

To his friends, Yamamoto did not attempt to disguise the truth. Time was running out, and he had begun to despair. He wrote to his old classmate from Etajima, Admiral Mitsumi Shimizu, the commander of the submarine fleet: "Guadalcanal was a very fierce battle. I do not know what to do next. Nor am I happy about facing my officers and men who have fought so hard without fear of death ... At the moment I would like to borrow some knowledge from a wise man."

5

The Hunters
Learn Their Trade

THE STENCH OF COPRA greeted the young men of
Henry Viccellio's 70th Fighter Squadron in the harbor at
Suva, and they saw the green Fijis through a heavy down-
pour of warm rain, a rain that seldom ceased for the next
few weeks.

At first the squadron lived in two-man tents beside a grass
strip at Nasouri, ten miles inland, struggling in foot-deep mud
as they uncrated their planes, twenty-four of the new Airacobras, sleek but slow fighters, heavily armored, ships which
could not fight at high altitudes. The crated planes were a
challenging puzzle to green crews, and were assembled only
by superhuman efforts of Harold Labounte, a factory representative from Bell Aircraft, who got them into the air
despite rain, ignorant crewmen and lack of moving equipment. By mid-February all the planes were in service and the
squadron moved across the island to a drier climate at
Nandi, and into comfortable quarters.

Life in the air was demanding. The 70th was a forgotten
squadron, for months largely independent of any command,
but the resourceful Viccellio scrounged targets, improvised
equipment and developed new techniques. Their gunnery
was limited to firing at ground targets, since their only tow
plane, an old Vickers Vincent, could not lift a target into the
air. But Viccellio's curriculum was thorough: instrument flying, acrobatics, gunnery, dive-and-skip-bombing.

The squadron was divided into flights, and began a fierce
competition. Lieutenant W. C. Sharpsteen led A Flight,
which included Tom Lanphier, and the Texans, Rivers and

50

Purnell. Mitchell led B Flight, "The Bearded Bastards of B," they called themselves, with Rex Barber and Doug Canning and Jack Jacobson among them. Barber flew as Mitchell's wingman for a time and then transferred to A Flight to join his Texas friends. The flights staged mock dogfights, tangling with a fury almost like that of combat. Mitchell keyed his men to a fighting pitch: "All right," he would yell, "let's go get those bastards today—they kept us awake all night!" and a lively scramble between A and B would follow—rat racing, Mitchell called it.

The pilots were sometimes wild, buzzing houses, blowing down the outrigger sailboats of native fishermen and driving people from bridges. Mitchell watched them more closely than they knew: "I tried to lead my guys on a loose rope. I knew you had to lead by example more than anything else. They watched what I did, and I tried my best in every way. So I couldn't just hand out orders. They were learning art as well as skill. I tried to make 'em aggressive, too. Good fighter pilots can't think defensively, I wanted to make 'em killers so that they could survive.

"I didn't mind if they got into fist fights or chased women —I just kept telling 'em they were the best. I approved a certain amount of wildness in them." The young men responded. When one of them had a narrow escape in the air, Mitchell would take him aside. "You came close today, boy. You've got to practice those slow rolls. I don't mean you shouldn't do 'em—but if you're going to roll, learn." There were no harsh reprimands.

When the reckless pilots shrugged off his advice, Mitchell said, "I don't mind losing you so much—but we can't stand to lose a plane."

"You mean to say a damned plane's worth more than I am?"

"Yeah, you're damned right it is."

The pilots invariably strode away, fuming, and practiced in a fury until he had perfected his roll.

The men of the 70th played as hard as they flew. Viccellio and Mitchell kept them at volleyball, softball and cricket in off hours, and the pilots devised recreation of their own, sometimes playing polo on gaunt island ponies.

Rex Barber became a casualty of a foray with the Texans. He and Rivers drove a 1933 Ford convertible about the island, powered by a motor taken from an old Army truck, and preyed upon the squardon's supplies for gasoline. During a gasoline raid one night Barber banged with a wooden mallet on a steel drum, and the mallet broke, smashed against his face and knocked out a tooth. He acquired a grin that was the envy of the squadron.

The pilots had occasional parties featuring a robust Australian beer or Dr. Stevens' medicinal alcohol, but their chief recreation was a perpetual poker game whose stakes became so high that some players ran up losses of $1000 in an evening, and the camp was full of IOU's passing as legal tender. Lanphier, Barber, Canning and Mitchell were usually winners. Jack Jacobson lost so heavily that he acquired a bodyguard—his creditors flew near him on every patrol and practice mission, for fear Japanese planes would somehow appear and shoot him down. Viccellio broke up the game when it reached a dangerous point, and ordered all IOU's canceled.

By now, after six months of training, the pilots had logged about four hundred hours in the air and were confident that they were finished fliers, ready for the enemy's best. It was the Navy which disillusioned them. The carrier *Saratoga* put her air group ashore on the Fijis soon after the battle of Midway, and for two weeks her fighter and bomber pilots trained Viccellio's men, giving them their final polishing for combat.

Many of the Navy pilots had fought at Midway, and were full of advice on gunnery and Japanese tactics. The most impressive of the newcomers was a big redhead, an exgunner's mate of about forty who had been promoted to ensign at Midway; he taught the men of the 70th how to shoot. A Navy plane towed a sleeve target for the Air Corps youngsters, while the big ensign and his pilots demonstrated firing.

The pilots also showed Viccellio's men how they had used their Wildcats in dogfights against the Japanese. The Navy fighters made tighter turns and climbed higher and faster than the cumbersome Airacobras and bested them in mock dogfights in the Fiji skies.* The carrier pilots taught them how to fight in pairs, scissoring back and forth in the Thach weave, a pattern which would keep the agile Zeroes off their tails.

---

* The fliers were soon to learn that Japanese combat pilots preferred to meet Airacobras above all other U.S. fighters.

Though the Navy veterans had much to teach the untested pilots of Nandi, they were astonished by the daring of Mitchell's men. The red-haired ensign watched the Bearded Bastards of B Flight wistfully as they roared over the field in tight formation, rolling and turning in their acrobatic drill. "By God, I'd like to have them aboard. If they live through it with their first Nips, they're going to give somebody hell compounded."

Mitchell and Barber and Lanphier and Canning and their mates saw the Navy leave with real regret.

In early autumn, as the 70th neared the end of its rear-area training, Lanphier became the first of the squadron to get a glimpse of the enemy and a taste of combat. Viccellio sent him by cargo plane to the island base of Espiritu Santo on a liaison mission, and while he was there Lanphier volunteered to go on a bombing mission with Colonel Blondy Saunders' Flying Fortresses. The four-plane flight spotted a small Japanese task force north of the Solomons, and dropped bombs, which missed badly. Several Zeroes flashed by, and Lanphier took a turn at the machine guns, helping to drive off the enemy. One Zero was downed, and Lanphier was credited with the kill—at least in the admiring 70th Squadron.

By now the Fijis had become a way point for VIP's on their way to Australia, and the 70th entertained several dignitaries. Captain Eddie Rickenbacker landed at Nandi, a walking skeleton fresh from his rescue after a crash landing at sea. The World War ace had survived twenty-four days of torture on a raft, and made the Fijis the first stop as he resumed his tour of air bases. Viccellio showed him about, and found the Captain interested in all details of their operation. Rickenbacker was so badly dehydrated that he carried a gallon jug of water wherever he went, even if he moved only a few steps.

The squadron had other important visitors. Commander Lyndon B. Johnson, a lanky Texas Congressman, came for two or three days as the emissary of President Roosevelt, and insisted upon seeing everything. He caught a bad cold during his stay and became seriously ill; Johnson was hospitalized with pneumonia in Australia a few days later.

High-ranking Air Corps officers also appeared—General George Kenney on his way to Port Moresby to head the 5th Air Force, and General H. H. Arnold, the Chief, on a tour of inspection to see for himself what the advanced units needed for combat. He got an enthusiastic greeting from A Flight —Barber and the Texans buzzed so low over the hotel that several Washington dignitaries fell to the floors as the fighters skimmed above the roof.

Arnold talked with pilots who complained to him about the clumsy P-39's. "Just be patient," he said. "We've known from the start that we'd have to give away speed for all that armor—but the day will come when you'll thank God for armor, and to hell with extra speed. We're beginning to learn how to handle the Zeros now, because they're absolutely naked—no protection, and they're gone at the first burst of fire."

Arnold also promised them better planes. "I can't tell you when, but your plane's on the way. You wait until you get in the saddle of a P-38. It's got power and speed and armor and range and guns, it climbs with the best of them and fights at any altitude you like. We'll show the Japs what a real fighter looks like."

They had been seven months in Fijis, drilling daily and flying their endless patrols in search of enemy reconnaissance planes which never came, when orders came to send fifteen of the most experienced pilots to New Caledonia, where they would stay for a few weeks to stage for Guadalcanal. Viccellio called in Mitchell.

"They're as ready as any squadron I ever saw," he said. "Now it's just a matter of keeping them up until they get into it."

Mitchell left with B Flight, which now included Sharpsteen and Doug Canning and Jack Jacobson and Jim McLanahan, and Mitchell's closest friend in the squadron, Wallace Dinn. The envious Lanphier and Barber and the rowdy Texans jeered them loudly as they left—but they were soon to follow. The quiet days on the Fijis had ended.

LIFE WAS GOOD FOR MITCHELL'S MEN in their few weeks on New Caledonia. They were assigned to the 67th Squadron and flew P-39's and P-400's, the latter an export model of the Airacobra intended for the British, of which a few found their way to the South Pacific. They found a

French hotel near their base where they could trade Spam for good meals of fresh chicken or pork, and there were American nurses in a hospital, to be wooed with fresh eggs and wine and the music of an old Victrola in the hotel.

Men who came back from the front gave Mitchell his first serious problem of morale. Survivors of a squadron mauled by the Japanese carrier pilots in the Solomons battles came through with tales of enemy supermen in super-planes. Mitchell was still indignant twenty-five years later; "They told my guys hairy stories. They said you were dead if a Zero got on your tail. They'd been chased off other islands and then got clobbered at Guadalcanal and were low in morale."

Mitchell called his men together. "All right," he said, "any of you guys who believe that crap from that new squadron, let me know it." The pilots were astonished to see that he was genuinely angry.

"I mean it," Mitchell said. "The road forks right here. Don't you believe one goddamn word they say. It's pure unadulterated horseshit. They haven't really fought Zeroes—but you sure as God will. If any of you think we can't lick Japs, say it now, and you can stay right here. Nobody's going with me who can't cut the mustard." No one spoke, and Mitchell was apparently satisfied, but for many days he drilled at them: "You're hot and getting hotter. You can handle anything that flies, if you stick to our team work. You're great pilots, and don't forget it."

Mitchell saw that he was reaching them: "Within a few days they just couldn't wait to get into combat." It was just in time. Viccellio flew to New Caledonia that week with orders:

"Mitch, they've asked for volunteers to go up to the Canal. Replacements. They're grinding 'em up over there."

"Count us in, Vic."

"Hadn't you better talk to 'em?"

Mitchell called the men of his contingent and said casually: "Vic wants Guadalcanal volunteers. But take it easy. If you all volunteer, I'll have to take my choice. How many?"

The pilots held up their hands.

"Okay," Mitchell said. "I can take only eight: Canning, Jacobson, Dinn, Gillon, Farron, Ramp, Shaw, Stern. We go up tonight."

JUST AFTER DAWN OF OCTOBER 5, 1942, Doug Canning saw Guadalcanal, the first of Mitchell's brood to see the grim landscape where they were to fight for seven months, and where half of the first contingent would die. Canning flew up from Noumea in a C-47 seated beside John Hersey, a young correspondent also entering his first active theater; they talked for an hour or so, but had fallen quiet when the plane neared the end of its run.

Below them pillars of gray smoke rose from the jungle encircling Henderson Field, the breakfast fires of the enemy. "God, it's spooky," Canning said. As they neared the field he saw charred and battered palm groves; the nearby beach was a ruin of rusted wrecks of planes, trucks and landing barges.

The control tower left by the Japanese was still in use, a crude unpainted wooden box on stilts. Nearby was a captured enemy truck on which a siren had been mounted—the alarm system for air raids. Canning met Mitchell and Jacobson and the others as they flew in from New Caledonia, and the pilots were taken to their new camp, a scattering of tents amid a junkyard, which was cut by zigzag trenches. Scarlet and white birds shrieked between the splintered trees, and hundreds of dirty, bearded and gaunt Marines roosted about the edge of the grove, regarding the new arrivals without interest. Beyond, in the coastal jungle and the towering hills of the interior, was enemy country. Thirty yards from Mitchell's tent a battery of Marine mortars fired sporadically during the day, the *whump! whump!* of the shells shaking his cot with each round.

Mitchell reported to the dugout headquarters of General A. A. Vandegrift, a Marine commander who, among his other duties, directed the tiny mixed air force of Navy, Marine, Army and New Zealand pilots which was to defend the Solomons. A Marine major greeted Mitchell and directed him to the post of Captain Dale Brannon, the commander of the new 339th Squadron, to which Mitchell's men now belonged—they were to fly in the old 70th no longer.

The newcomers met another pilot with whom they would fly for the next month—Besby Holmes of the 67th, who had arrived here three days earlier. The new pilots were amused by Holmes, a lean, laughing boy with a thin black mustache, full of tales of Pearl Harbor, where he had been caught in the enemy attack.

The enemy gave the new pilots a fiery welcome that night.

A light explosion burst overhead at about one o'clock, and a star shell drifted into the palms, shedding a sickly green light; the grove erupted with explosions, with palms bursting and crashing, and the wounded screaming above the din.

Jack Jacobson dashed for the big dugout, collided with a man at the entrance, and both fell to the ground, stunned, but crawled down the sandbagged entrance. The place was packed with men. Doug Canning scrambled from the side of his tent, still half asleep, running wildly; when he realized that he was lost he retraced his steps, ducked back into the tent, and out its front flaps to the dugout. Terrified, he squeezed into the mass and lay against the wall as the shells burst overhead. Men retched, but no one thought of moving for an hour and a half, while the shells searched the grove. Japanese warships stood close inshore, hammering the field and the camp.

Men crawled to the surface during a lull and found the grove lit by burning planes. Two Marine pilots and two infantrymen were dead. The Japanese came again the next night, firing with the same fury, and the Air Corps pilots and the Marines lived in the holes for two days, eating little or nothing. They emerged to find the coral covered with shrapnel, the grove torn to splinters—and all but nine of the sixty planes of Henderson Field destroyed. The wrecks were hurriedly shoved aside, Seabees in their old Japanese trucks and rollers went to work on the steel mat which covered the pocked runway, and mechanics swarmed over the salvageable planes. A few F4F's and four P-39's were found to be in flying condition, but the field was closed to bombers for more than a month.

There was almost no gas the morning after the shelling, but Jacobson siphoned a few gallons from an abandoned B-17 and flew his first mission with a half-filled tank, scrambling with a few others in response to a false alarm of approaching enemy planes. Japanese infantry fired at him as he took off. Their lines were only six hundred feet from the eastern end of the runway. Jacobson landed with his tank almost empty, thinking that he had made his final flight, since the enemy was closing in.

The Marine major from headquarters found Mitchell on the line: "How much gas you got left, Captain?"

"About twelve drums," Mitchell said.

"Well, fly it out, and that's it. We figure they're coming

after the field now. They're landing reinforcements down the beach every night. When your gas is gone, get your men together and put 'em in line along here."

Mitchell joined his mechanics and pilots in stripping .30 caliber machine guns from the planes, formed the men into firing teams, and at nightfall made ready for a last-ditch defense. Cargo planes saved them in the morning, C-47's hauling in gasoline.

Guadalcanal seemed lost by mid-October. The enemy's strength on the island was now estimated at about 29,000 troops, the Marines were hard-pressed at the perimeter, and Henderson Field was almost useless.

From the west, at Rabaul, the Japanese hammered at the Solomons in an effort to dislodge the Americans. Guadalcanal was their particular target, and Henderson Field was the bull's-eye. Mitchell and his pilots retreated from their tents to burrows in a bluff over the Tenaru River, where they squiggled down in the sand to sleep, and lived on atabrine, C-rations and wormy Japanese rice. The crew chiefs slept under the planes, ready to fight for them in case of an enemy breakthrough.

On one of the most hectic of these days Japanese bombers came over Henderson Field at 17,000 feet, showering their bombs from beyond the reach of the P-400's. The historian of the 67th wrote: "All the 67th could do was fly around, helpless. Discouraged, they went back to land. The whole field seemed to be afire. Grass was burning, two hangars built by the Japs were afire, several airplanes were burning and ammunition was exploding in every direction." Men swarmed on the runway, which seemed to be sprouting with bushes—they were being held in place to mark craters for incoming planes, the men holding the bushes as long as they dared during the approach of the fighters, which then zigzagged down the strip, dodging holes. Trucks hauled dirt and coral to fill the craters, men beat out grass fires with their blankets—their only blankets. Litter bearers trotted in and out, bearing the wounded. Crews rolled gas and oil drums to the planes, which were refueled by hand, and men shoveled dirt on burning planes, daring death from explosions. From across the Lunga River Japanese snipers took a steady toll.

The squadron historian added in unscholarly indignation:

"All worked in a silent fury at the enemy. But what could the 67th do in its damned P-400's?"

Amid this confusion, missions against the enemy were still flown regularly by the airmen of Cactus, as Guadalcanal was known in the current code. Wallace Dinn flew a few miles up the coast and dropped a bomb into the hold of a beached Japanese transport and blew it apart, flinging hundreds of bodies high into the air. He was the first of the Air Corps pilots to strike at the enemy reinforcements on the beaches; he flew through anti-aircraft fire untouched, to return to the field, but most pilots were not so lucky.

Night landings cost the 339th several men and planes. The half dozen dim lights of the strip were obscured by frequent storms sweeping the island. Mitchell often found his way in only by a line of phosphorescent light as the waves broke on the beach below, landing on the rough strip in rain so blinding he could not see through the windscreen, and sideslipped downward in order to see out one side of the cockpit.

The struggle to save Guadalcanal was even more desperate than the pilots knew. Secretary Knox, in a Washington press conference on October 16, was asked whether Guadalcanal could be held: "I certainly hope so. I expect so. I don't want to make any predictions, but every man out there, ashore or afloat will give a good account of himself." In the same week Admiral Nimitz sent Admiral William Halsey to command in the South Pacific, saying that "the critical situation requires a more aggressive commander." From that time, the tide began to turn. It was long imperceptible on Guadalcanal.

In the night of October 24–25 the Japanese made their supreme effort to overrun Henderson Field, but though they threw a full division against Colonel Chesty Puller's half-strength Marine battalion, they were slaughtered. Action was so heavy that machine gunners urinated in the water jackets of overheated guns to keep them firing, and men had to push down walls of Japanese bodies so that gunners could continue to fire. A Marine took John Mitchell to the edge of the jungle to show him the 1400 corpses lying along the Marine barbed wire. Mitchell had already flown two missions that day, the sun was hot and the bodies had begun to decompose. Mitchell could eat no breakfast.

Mitchell's leadership was already helping to make the 339th Squadron effective. He shot down his first Zero four days after he arrived, added another less than two weeks later, and a third in the first week of November. He was well on his way to becoming an ace. Unlike some officers who had been heros to their squadrons in training, Mitchell seemed to thrive on combat; he exuded confidence and was important to the morale of the command. He was still only a flight leader, but men looked up to him as the natural leader of the squadron. The men quickly learned that Mitchell was fearless.

Early one morning he led P-39's on an escort mission to Bougainville, escorting Flying Fortresses as they bombed the Japanese airfield at Kahili. On the way home he spotted a swarm of Zeros and took his flight after them, though they did not menace the bombers. They shot down five of the enemy, but when they returned, Mitchell discovered that his friend Dinn had been shot down. Soon after he learned of the loss, while he was tired and breakfastless and depressed at the death of his friend, Mitchell was upbraided for the loss of Dinn by General D. C. Strother of Fighter Command. His pilots stood open-mouthed as Mitchell snapped angrily at Strother, saying that they had brought the bombers in safely, had always done their best to save men, and regretted Dinn's loss more than anyone on the island, of whatever rank.

Mitchell went to Strother soon afterward to apologize: "I was half starved and nervous, I was sore, and Dinn was my best buddy, I'm sorry I flew off the handle."

"O.K., Mitch," Strother said. "I realize you were upset. Just don't ever forget how precious men and machines are out here now. See that they don't take unnecessary chances."

Pilots added the incident to the stock of Mitchell lore as evidence that he would stand up to anyone for the sake of his men, and that he was respected by the high command.

It was almost inevitable that Mitchell would become a squadron commander, and in November, when Dale Brannon went out, he took over the 339th. He was also promoted to major. His rise was almost obscured by the arrival of the Lightnings.

They came on November 12, a dozen of the huge twin-tailed fighters, sweeping down on Henderson Field between rows of ragged troops of all services, men who waved their caps and cheered. The enemy was to be met on equal terms at last, and the months of improvised defense were over. The 339th still flew some of the P-39's and P-400's, but it was now classed as a twin-engine squadron, the first in the Pacific.

Mitchell was the first of the squadron to get into a Lightning. He fell in love with the new plane. He could hardly believe his ears when the powerful Allison engines broke into a roar on either side of him, turning up their 1350 horsepower.

Its handling in the air was astonishingly smooth. He clambered out after flight, shouting to his men, "It ain't a goddam rattrap at all. We'll clobber 'em now—it's just like moving from a Model T to a Cadillac."

The P-38, the first U.S. twin-engine fighter, had a top speed of 395 miles an hour at 25,000 feet, a ceiling almost unlimited, and devastating firepower. Its four .50 caliber machine guns and a 20 millimeter cannon were mounted in the nose, with an unobstructed field of fire; the guns carried 2000 rounds and the cannon a maximum of 120 shells. The weapons were mounted to shoot straight ahead, so that they could shoot down opponents at long range.* The big ships could also carry a 1000 pound bomb, half as much as a Flying Fortress.

The pilots had heard stories of the Lightning as a mankiller in its tests in California, of the difficulty of bailing out, of its tendency to buffet or tear itself apart in a steep dive, but the men of the 339th found the fighters superb. Mitchell led practice dogfights against other planes of the command: "We felt pretty cocky those first days, and when we saw P-39's or P-40's we'd bounce 'em for practice. They'd just be sitting there, thinking about going home or something, and a plane would zoom right down on them. It was scary, and it taught 'em to keep a watch." The pilots of the 339th found that they could outdistance other planes rapidly in shallow climbs at high speed; the Zero might be more maneuverable, but it was not nearly so powerful or tough as the Lightning.

The planes had imperfections: pilots who left the heat of Guadalcanal and soared to a chilly 30,000 feet suffered from cramps; the feeble heaters did not keep men warm, and if pilots dressed for high altitudes, they roasted below; the ships consumed gasoline at an appalling rate, especially in

---

* A great advantage over other fighters of the day, whose guns were bore-sighted, giving them converging fields of fire about 250 yards in front of the plane, thus limiting their range.

combat or at low altitude, and the spare gas tanks they carried beneath the wings, to be dropped in dogfights, were always in short supply; instruments were quickly affected by the tropical climate and some planes had to be stripped to keep others flying. All this was forgiven, for the men of the 339th thought the Lightning was the finest fighter in the world.

Mitchell developed combat tactics for the big plane, based on four-ship sections flying together in a "ball" within a one-mile radius, for mutual protection.

The P-38's were too large to weave back and forth in pairs in combat, but Mitchell found that they were deadly when diving after Zeroes. Since they were slower than the Zeroes on turns, Mitchell's men learned to turn under the enemy in pursuit, and then catch them in high-speed climbs. With skillful use of flaps, they could turn inside almost any plane in the Pacific.

The new ship was also a wonder to the enemy. A captured Japanese pilot was allowed to get into the gondola of a Lightning at Fighter Two one day while Mitchell's men watched his reactions. The enemy flier, who had once been a commerical pilot, looked about him wide-eyed, rapped on the big glass windscreen and on the steel floor, brushed his hand across the instrument panel, and gaped at the armament system. He gave a loud exclamation of wonder, but then told an interpreter, "We fear the P-38's much more than we fear the men who fly them." Mitchell's pilots roared with laughter as the bewildered prisoner was led away.

Japanese bombers no longer came over Guadalcanal with impunity, for the Lightnings brought a new day to the island's defenders. Zero pilots could not now sweep low over the field to draw off protecting fighters and leave the target open for their bombers, and enemy bombers were now unable to fly safely out of reach. Mitchell helped to devise the new defense: at the sound of raid alarms, all the field's fighters scrambled—the Lightnings went to 30,000 feet, the Navy and Marine F4U's to 25,000, with the Wildcats, Airacobras and P-40 Tomahawks below at about 12,000. The scores of planes waited, stacked in position, ready to dive on Zero and bomber formations and scatter them for dogfights. The toll of Japanese planes rose sharply.

Mitchell also helped to end the nightly nuisance raids of Washing Machine Charlie, an enemy bomber pilot who woke up the airmen about midnight with the *whang-whang* whine of his unsynchronized engines, followed by the crack of a small bomb. He aroused anti-aircraft crews, who blazed at him ineffectually, even when he was caught in the glare of searchlights. Despite weeks of pleading, Mitchell was refused permission to stalk Charlie with his P-38, and one night in December he went up without orders, waited for Charlie to appear, located him with the aid of the control tower, and shot him down in flames. The appreciative audience watching from tents and foxholes below broke into cheers, and Mitchell became a hero of the command; later, other pilots shot down a few of Charlie's successors, and the defenders slept undisturbed.

In December the pilots of the old 70th Squadron met again. Viccellio brought up a new group, among them Tom Lanphier and Rex Barber. They did not fly with Mitchell's men, since the squadrons alternated on duty, but they lived together at Fighter Number Two, often used the same planes in rotation, and exchanged information from missions against the enemy. All of the pilots, even the newcomers, looked to Mitchell for leadership.

"Mitch talked sense, and only from experience," Barber recalled. "He had a very direct and earnest manner, and we all knew he was hot in combat. We could sense that he was telling us only what was true, and that it might make the difference between life and death."

Lanphier said, "Mitchell was given credit by the command for keeping up the morale of the flying people. You heard more about Joe Foss and Smith and the other Marines, but Mitch was every bit as good. He was a real fighting pilot."

The newcomers of the 70th quickly established themselves. Lanphier shot down his first Zero on Christmas Eve, almost directly over the field. Two days later he led a sweep against an airfield on New Georgia Island, downing two Zeroes and strafing the field. His flight left supply dumps and gasoline tanks burning, and destroyed twelve planes, a mission for which Lanphier was given the DFC. His mates admired his coolness in combat. One day when he spotted a freighter in the sea near Guadalcanal he called to others of his flight and arranged a pool, each man to contribute five dollars, with the pot to be taken by the flier with the best shot. Lanphier quickly went down, dropped a 500-pound bomb on the freighter's deck and sank her. He collected thirty dollars.

Viccellio's entire squadron was led at a relentless pace. In one busy month his pilots averaged sixty-five hours of combat time per man. Viccellio did not lose a man in his long tour of duty on Guadalcanal, the only such squadron with a flawless record. His men shot down seventy enemy planes in this tour.

Other pilots also won attention. Rex Barber, oblivious to an escort of Zeroes, shot down a big bomber just as it was landing on New Georgia Island, and got a Silver Star for the feat. This mission appealed to Mitchell, and from that time he and Barber became fast friends. "Only one thing mattered to Mitch," Barber said. "You had to be there when you were needed."

Jacobson also won a Silver Star for one of his first missions, on which he fought Zeroes at high altitude until his oxygen gave out, then dived to strafe enemy transports on the beach below, knocking out several anti-aircraft guns. On the same day, with eight others, he attacked a Japanese fleet of five transports and eight destroyers, and scored one direct hit.

Doug Canning went into his first combat without having fired the guns of his P-38, and he was astonished to see how effective the fire was; he got on the tail of a Zero at about 6000 feet, over Kahili, and exploded it with one short burst.

There were other competent pilots—Joe Moore and Jim McLanahan, D. C. Goerke and Ray Hine, the latter a handsome blond boy from Indianapolis who was a favorite with his mates.

The men of the Air Corps squadrons developed a close camaraderie in their tents and burrows on the hill overlooking Fighter Number Two. Their six-week tours were almost unbroken rounds of flying patrols or scrambling for defense by day. They spent much of their spare time helping line crews work over their planes, to which they became attached. Several of the Lightnings bore names—Mitchell's was "Mitch's Squitch," inspired by a demonic comic-strip character of the day; Lanphier's was "Phoebe," for his fiancée; Barber's was "Diablo."

In the nights there was little for the pilots to do but sleep, join bull sessions or listen to records. From Canning's tent they often heard the worn favorite "Harbor Lights" and "He Wore a Pair of Silver Wings." Barber's prized record was "Take It Off—Take It Off," a ballad about "Queenie, the Cutie of the Burlesque Show."

Late in the year a small U.S.O. library opened on the

island and the pilots amused themselves by searching out books of humor, not to read, but to take to Besby Holmes—to hear him shout with laughter as he lay in his cot, an infectious bray that soon put the whole camp to laughing.

The men seemed to have lost the gambling fever which had raged on the Fijis, and there were few games of poker or blackjack. The ceaseless strain of the war against the Japanese seemed to sap their energies.

On January 1, 1943, Mitchell took stock of the record of the 339th: twenty-one enemy planes shot down, plus seven probables. Four of his pilots had been killed in combat and half a dozen in accidents. The squadron's dive bombing and strafing had helped to slow the Japanese offensive. Guadalcanal seemed safe. The First Marines had left in December, and the action moved westward as the Americans began to strike toward Rabaul.

Mitchell came down with malaria and went into a hospital on New Caledonia for a few weeks; he also took a week of leave in Australia, but was soon back on duty. Viccellio was promoted to headquarters of the new 13th Fighter Command at Noumea, and afterward shuttled between New Caledonia and Guadalcanal.

In February the fliers got a commander of their own, Admiral Charles Mason, who came as chief of the newly created Air Command, Solomons, which was only a new name for the small mixed air force of Army, Navy, Marine and New Zealand fliers, at last recognized and given a place on command charts.

The pace of the air war quickened in March. One day Barber, Lanphier, Joe Moore and two others blew up seven Japanese float planes near Shortland Island, and on the way home found an enemy destroyer far from base and all alone. They swept down, strafing and bombing, and Barber whizzed over so closely that he ripped forty-two inches off one wing of his plane on the ship's stack, but still flew 210 miles home to safety and made a normal landing. The pilots were given Silver Stars or clusters for the mission, one of the few on which fighters sank a destroyer.

High-ranking officers came visiting almost daily, now that there was no danger from sniper fire. Secretary of the Navy Frank Knox appeared and rode about on an inspection, stopping his jeep now and then to bellow brief patriotic speeches to pilots and infantrymen, who stared at him in astonishment. The command sent up more than one hundred planes to guard him as he came in and departed from Henderson Field.

As April came in word leaked from intelligence at Admiral Mason's headquarters that the enemy was beginning to stir.

6

"I Am Studying Strategy Just Now"

SHOCK WAVES OF THE JAPANESE DEFEAT at Guadalcanal moved up the island battlefields through the Bismarcks
and to Rabaul in New Britain, from where the campaign had
been launched.

The new capital of the Southeast Area lay in a forbidding
landscape, an island whose uplands were drowned under two
hundred inches of rainfall each year, a rugged, unexplored
jumble of hills and rain forests, humid and unhealthy. Its
insects, reptiles and animals were often more menacing than
the enemy—spiders as large as dinner plates, disease-bearing
ticks and mosquitoes, wasps three inches long, centipedes,
scorpions and leeches, crocodiles and giant boa constrictors.
Rabaul had been captured a year earlier from the Australians
—who were abandoning it after the eruption of a volcano
that towered above its harbor.

But it was now the anchor of the Japanese position in the
south, the post from which Yamamoto still hoped to cut the
long Allied supply line and to invade Australia itself. As
spring came to the comfortable, well-established base at
Truk, it became apparent that Isoroku Yamamoto would soon
visit the uninviting outpost at Rabaul. A long-delayed coun-
teroffensive in the area was now possible; the planes were at
hand. In March, Japanese plane production reached five
hundred a month for the first time. Tokyo ordered Yamamoto
to the south.

The Commander in Chief was convinced that divided command had cost Japan the Guadalcanal campaign, and saw
that the struggle between the Army and Navy was intensify-

ing. The Army now built cargo ships and submarines in its own shipyards; the Navy had its own motor corps for land transport. The services fought savagely over control of industrial plants. Japan now had three separate weather observatories, Army, Navy and civilian. Differences over strategy threatened ruin.

Thus Yamamoto was delighted when his old friend, Lieutenant General Hitoshi Imamura, appeared in Truk on his way to take command of the 8th Field Army in Rabaul. Imamura came aboard the *Musashi* with news that the Army was sending two fresh divisions south, but Yamamoto urged him to press Tokyo for more men:

"We have lost heavily. Enemy air power is destroying our transport. When you reach Rabaul, please study the gap between American air power and our own. I hope you will ask for many more planes."

They dined with their staff officers aboard the flagship, and when they were alone Yamamoto's manner became solemn: "Times are changing, Hitoshi. When the war began, one of our fighter pilots was the equal of five Americans, but no more. We cannot deceive ourselves, or indulge our vanity.

"Since Midway things are not the same. We lost too many superior pilots, and from that day have not had adequate replacements."

"Are American pilots well trained by now?" Imamura asked.

Yamamoto was reluctant to concede superiority to the enemy. "It's possible that the longer they train, the greater their skill. But it is the machines—the planes—and not the men. Today it is a war of our superior training against American equipment."

Yamamoto talked of the problem until the General left the ship; Imamura saw that it had been preying upon his mind: "It may seem that we have a ratio of no worse than one or two against the enemy, but since the American replacement rate is three times our own, their superiority in numbers of planes grows each day. So we fight an enemy many times our own strength. We are in a difficult time.

"I now realize that our people have not advanced in the scientific field. They need that as well as spiritual power. I feel a terrible responsibility for this; the air forces have been my charge for so long."

As the General left the ship Yamamoto brightened and

called a cheery farewell and promised to do all in his power to help beat back the American thrust westward through the Solomons.

In March, 1943, after the surface Navy had suffered a disastrous defeat in the Battle of the Bismarck Sea, only 300 Japanese planes remained in the vast Southeast Area, 200 of them Navy planes. Tokyo refused reinforcements to replace Imamura's losses, and American bombers flew over his bases almost at will.

In late March Yamamoto advised his area commander at Rabaul, Vice Admiral Jinichi Kusaka, that he was sending about three hundred planes from four carriers of the 3rd Fleet, based at Truk, so that the reinforced Army and Navy squadrons could pound Allied positions in the Solomons and New Guinea and destroy American air power in the area. He sent staff officers to Rabaul in advance with details of a plan he called I Operation, which was to open with one heavy blow against harbors and airfields at Tulagi and Guadalcanal.

Yamamoto flew to Rabaul on April 3, the day before the new operation was to begin. He found it an enormous base, surpassing even Truk, ringed by five airfields, an expansive harbor filled with ships, and nearly 100,000 men in its complex of camps, fields and navy posts. Rabaul also boasted the fanciest brothel east of the Dutch East Indies, with some six hundred Japanese and Korean women to serve officers and men.

A turnout of several hundred greeted Yamamoto at the airfield and escorted him to Headquarters, a collection of dingy wooden buildings, where visiting commanders and their staffs were crowded into Admiral Kusaka's office. Most of the squadrons were scattered among outlying bases near Bougainville, but the swollen command staff taxed facilities in Rabaul. The bedlam increased the next day, when storms forced a postponement of the offensive. For three days rains lashed New Britain and grounded Japanese planes.

Yamamoto's quarters were at some distance from Headquarters, in a cottage on a quiet hilltop, but he seldom saw the place. He bustled about the island, inspecting airfields and hangars and hurrying into hospitals, where he greeted every man in the wards, repeating at each bed his earnest words: "I deeply appreciate what you have endured for our country. Please recover soon and let us meet again at sea. Please take care of yourself." Among his staff he was jolly and high-spirited, and enjoyed the good meals at Headquarters, which were prepared from delicacies flown down from Japan.

The commander seemed to miss nothing. Captain Yoshio Miwa, a senior aide on Admiral Kusaka's, staff, was not feeling well, but attended meetings with Yamamoto despite a high temperature. Yamamoto often urged him to go to bed, and at luncheon or supper he invariably sent to Miwa's table a piece of fresh melon from his private stock. Yamamoto continued to badger Miwa about taking care of himself until he agreed to go to the hospital for treatment.

Kusaka, who had not become accustomed to the tropics, suffered from dysentery and sat about glumly as they ate. Yamamoto teased him, "Ah no, Kusaka. It's not the jungle air. It's that insatiable appetite. You eat too much." He was fond of Kusaka, one of his most gifted commanders and a kinsman of Ryunosuke Kusaka, who had helped to plan the Pearl Harbor attack. The talk at meals and at informal sessions afterward was so casual that only an occasional respectful "*Gensui*" by a subordinate gave a hint that Yamamoto was present.

Before dawn of April 7 the dive bombers took off from Rabaul to join the planes massing at Ballale for the opening of the offensive. The last glimpse of the base for the pilots was the stocky figure of Yamamoto, impeccable in his whites, vigorously waving his cap in circles overhead.

The first blow was a heavy one: 188 planes—117 Zeroes and 71 dive bombers—droned eastward toward the cluster of Allied ships in the harbors of Guadalcanal and Tulagi. They flew down the island chain without fear of interception, the largest attack force yet sent down the Slot.

As Yamamoto's planes came near, fighters of every description rose from Henderson Field, and the battle raged for three hours in the skies between the Russell Islands and Guadalcanal, a violent crackling action that flung the planes across more than 250 square miles in a skein of dogfights. Some of the dive bombers got through and slammed at ships in Tulagi Harbor. The Japanese flew home.

The Rabaul contingent put down at its airfield to find Yamamoto there, smiling proudly and waving the white cap as if he had not changed his post all day. The flight leaders had exciting reports, and when all bases had been heard from, Yamamoto's officers gave him a misleading summary of the day's action: only about ten U.S. planes, Grummans and P-38's, had come up to meet them, and were beaten back; twenty-six warships had been bombed in Tulagi Harbor, most of them sunk.

Twenty-one Japanese planes had been lost.

The toll was high, but since Headquarters accepted the reports of damage to enemy shipping at face value, the staff was elated. Yamamoto, convinced that Guadalcanal had been crippled, turned his attention to other American-held islands. Just before each new strike was launched, the pilots based at Rabaul were assembled in front of Headquarters, where a large, chalk-smeared blackboard listed the name of each man, with his most recent tally of enemy ships and planes. The men stood patiently in their flying gear as Yamamoto exhorted them to press home their attacks and block the enemy drive against the Japanese stronghold in the southeast.

On April 11 a fleet of ninety-four fighter and bombers struck in Oro Bay, near Burma in New Guinea, and reported four Allied ships sunk and twenty-one planes shot down, at a cost of only six Japanese planes.

On April 12 Yamamoto sent 174 raiders to Port Moresby, the New Guinea headquarters of Douglas MacArthur and George Kenney; returning pilots claimed twenty-eight Allied planes destroyed, a transport sunk, and the airfield badly damaged.

Yamamoto's aides noticed that he was in remarkably high spirits as I Operation reach a climax. Kusaka and several other officers, classmates at Etajima in their days as midshipmen, planned a reunion party on April 13, and the *Gensui* invited himself, appearing with two bottles of Johnny Walker Scotch as a contribution, and leading the crowd in laughing recollections of their naval careers; Yamamoto had been an officer on the square-rigged sailing ship in which they had cruised around the world in their final year at the academy. At his suggestion they all signed a letter of greetings to their old comrades, a letter written in Yamamoto's accomplished calligraphy.

On that day, from the seaplane base at Shortland Island off Bougainville, the itinerary of Yamamoto's forthcoming tour of the advanced bases was sent to commanders throughout the area. The *Gensui* would travel on Sunday morning, leaving Rabaul at 6 A.M., to visit Ballale, Buin and Shortland. The message went out in top-security code, signed by Vice

Admiral Tomoshige Samejima, the new commander of the 8th Air Fleet.

I Operation came to an end the following day, April 4, with a raid on Milne Bay and a nearby airfield. The pilots said they had inflicted heavy damage—ten U.S. transports sunk and forty-four planes downed. By April 16 all the flight leaders had come in, and there was a day of celebration and congratulation.

Allied losses in the operation, Admiral Ugaki announced, were extremely heavy: one cruiser, two destroyers, twenty-five transports and 134 planes. They had lost forty-two planes themselves.*

I Operation was a huge success, Ugaki said, and the personal leadership of the Commander in Chief had been inspiring. The staff would spend the next day planning future campaigns, and on Sunday, Yamamoto would tour the front-line bases, to congratulate the fighting men who had won the victories in the air.

JUNIOR OFFICERS HAD HARDLY A GLIMPSE of the commander on April 17; conferences began in the early morning and continued until nightfall. Dozens of officers thronged Headquarters, and Yamamoto presided over each session, weighing unit reports from the I Operation, hearing conflicting estimates on their needs from Army and Navy commanders, and urging each of them to prepare specific plans to contain the enemy advance along the island chain. He carried much of the work himself, since Ugaki was feverish and spent the day in bed; Yamamoto studied the reports as he dealt with each group of officers. The reports of Navy commanders from the forward bases were not reasuring; the officers bickered and charged each other with tolerating a low state of morale in their squadrons. Watanabe saw that the Admiral was weary at the end of the day, when he went to his quarters for a quiet meal. They ate alone.

There was a growing uneasiness among the staff about the

---

* At this time the Allies reported their losses in all I Operation raids as one destroyer, one tanker, one corvette, two Dutch merchant ships and twenty-five planes; they estimated that fifty-one Japanese planes had been shot down.

flight of the next day, but Yamamoto laughed and dismissed warnings of danger. At lunch Imamura had told him a long story of his own narrow escape at Bougainville, when American planes had tried to ambush him between the coast and the mountains, but the pilot had luckily escaped into the clouds.*

"Yes," Yamamoto said. "They are penetrating our front, and we must stop them. That is one reason I am flying there tomorrow—with plenty of cover, Hitoshi. Please don't concern yourself about me."

In the afternoon there was a more insistent plea. Rear Admiral Takoji Joshima, the commander of the 11th Air Fleet, flew in from Bougainville to urge that the flight be canceled. His air of urgency alarmed younger officers:

"I told my staff when I saw that foolish message that this was madness. This is an open invitation to the enemy—I would never permit such recklessness from my headquarters."

When he saw Yamamoto, Joshima urged him to change the plan. "Please. This is dangerous. We no longer have rear bases there; it is the front line. I know conditions."

Yamamoto smiled. "What is this between you and Imamura? A conspiracy? Don't be so fanciful. There is no cause for alarm. Even if it were dangerous, I could not turn back. I've told all these people, here, there and everywhere, all over the place. They will be waiting for me."

He threw an arm around Joshima's shoulders. "I'll be back, all right. We leave in the morning, quite early, and return in the evening. You must have dinner with me tomorrow night."

Some of this talk reached Kusaka, who was also busy in the conferences, and was unable to see Yamamoto. He spoke with Kuroshima: "If there is danger, and he won't give up the flight, I can furnish all the fighters he needs—six will not be enough if there is going to be trouble. Please tell Ugaki."

Kuroshima did not see Ugaki, and Kusaka's message was not delivered.

Yamamoto played *shogi* with Watanabe in his room after

---

* P-38's from Guadalcanal had made several previous flights to Bougainville, usually on bomber escort or strafing missions—but they had never flown a full-scale fighter sweep in great strength. They usually lacked sufficient extra gas tanks to assure the big fighters the range.

dinner and once interrupted the play: "I want you to stay here tomorrow and finish the conference. If we don't pull them together now, we're in trouble. You know what to tell them, and make things very clear. We must go back to Truk as soon as we can."

There was a knock at the door and a duty officer called: "Can you see a visitor, sir?"

Yamamoto did not look up from the board: "Tell him I am studying strategy just now."

The Admiral went to bed before midnight, but slept little. His aides were passing through the Headquarters area most of the night. At the hospital Yoshio Miwa was also sleepless. Soon after 4 A.M. he went onto the veranda and sat to watch the dawn. He was surprised to see a young officer mount the steps, a beribboned young man in khaki fatigues, bring a message from Yamamoto:

"The commander regrets that he will be unable to see you for a while, but asks that you do not force yourself. Don't be impatient, and please take care of your health."

"Please say to him that I am better," Miwa said. "I will be discharged in a week or so."

Not long afterward Miwa watched idly as a small fleet of planes rose from the airfield below and roared across the bay—two bombers and several fighters.

7

"At All Costs
Reach and Destroy"

BEFORE DAWN OF APRIL 1 the radio dugout at Guadalcanal had word from Admiral Halsey's headquarters in New Caledonia that the new Commander Air, Solomons, was on his way. The new chief—"Air Mica" in the code—was Rear Admiral Marc Mitscher.

The morning's routine at Henderson Field began with a scramble. After breakfast four Wildcats took off to meet enemy dive bombers and about thirty Zeroes over the nearby Russell Islands, where the dive bombers hit the airfield and harbor.

The planes were still out and the red flag was flying when a plump PBY came in for a landing across Ironbottom Sound. A half-naked boy in the control tower yelled to a jeepload of officers parked in the shade below, "That's him," and the jeep rolled away on the skirt of the strip's roller coaster matting. Pete Mitscher crawled from the PBY.

Mitscher was slow to recognize the yellow-faced officer who came from the jeep to greet him—Admiral Charles Mason, an old friend to whom he had turned over the *Hornet* only ten months ago, and whom he now came to relieve. There were other officers, among them Lieutenant Colonel Viccellio and Marine Brigadier Field Harris, who was to be Mitscher's chief of staff. After a round of introductions they took the Admiral to his headquarters, pointing out the fighter strips and camps and other installations on the way.

Mitscher was still inspecting the place when eight Wildcats took off from Fighter Strip Number Two, hurrying westward before they got into formation. Mitscher gazed after them. "They're needing help at the Russells," someone said.

Mitscher was waiting at Fighter Two when the planes returned, and listened as the pilots were debriefed by intelligence officers. Only four of the reinforcement of Wildcats had made it back. The pilots said they had knocked down three Zeroes, and the dive bombers had gone away at last.

At noon Mitscher had Spam and dehydrated potatoes and a mug of weak tea, eating from a mess tray in his lap; there was no mess tent. He was still toying with his food when Fighter Two roared into life again. This time fifteen fighters went up, Lightnings and Grummans and Airacobras, and Mitscher watched them climb into position, stacked downward from 30,000 feet to await the Zeroes. The action lasted for half an hour or more, and several planes fell from the sky. The pilots reported thirteen Zeroes downed, with two losses of their own.

"This is a goddamn tiger pit," Mitscher said contentedly. "Like this every day?"

"It's a little light for a Thursday," Harris said, "but it'll pick up."

For the rest of the day Mitscher moved about alone, studying the lethargic, hollow-eyed, malarial men of the fighter command, few of whom looked up at his passage. He returned to Harris with the first orders: Halsey was to be sent urgent requests for galley equipment, mess plates, huts and decent food. They must have more gasoline and a supply of aircraft parts. The dispatches went out that night.

PETE MITSCHER had spent the past ten months ashore before he talked himself into this combat job, first as the despondent skipper of Patrol Wing 2, a flying boat outfit at Pearl Harbor. Mitscher complained that he would never see action and begged that he be returned to duty at sea, preferably into the battles for the Solomons, and at last, possibly because several junior admirals showed distaste for it, Mitscher was given the job at Guadalcanal.

"I knew we'd catch hell up there," Halsey said, "and that's why I sent Pete Mitscher. I knew he was a fighting fool."

The men of the ragged Cactus fighter command guessed it at once: Mitscher's dress was so plain that he was more than once mistaken for an overage chief petty officer. His parchment skin was always beaded in sweat, but he wore long khakis every day, as a defense against the mosquito swarms; his face was half-hidden by a long-billed baseball cap.

Pete Mitscher was fifty-six years old, and had spent thirty-seven years in the Navy, about half of the time at sea. No one in the service knew more about carriers and their planes. In 1916, aboard the cruiser *Huntington*, he had brought the first workable plane catapult into use; he flew one of the four NC-1's in the Navy's pioneer transatlantic flight in 1919, and made it to the Azores before his plane sank. He had been the first air officer of the first true American carrier, *Saratoga*, and landed the first plane on her deck.

Mitscher had always gone his own way, unassuming and plain, with a grim reserve. One writer who came to know him well on shipboard said that Mitscher had "a built-in gyroscopic resistance to the display of emotions under any circumstances."

The command quickly became accustomed to his taciturn ways, and delighted in seeing the grim contortion of his seamed face that greeted news good and bad, a death's head grimace known as The Guadalcanal Smile; it was this expression that came onto his face when he had a report that the enemy had tortured and executed some of Doolittle's pilots. The men quoted his soft growl: "I hate those goddamn yellow bastards worse than if I were a Marine."

They also liked the scuttlebutt they heard from his headquarters: when an air alert was sounded he never took shelter until five minutes before the bombs were supposed to fall, looking around to see how the command prepared to fight. Best of all, he carried no posse of staff officers with him, and was usually alone as he poked about the island, asking quiet questions of the men, an aviator's questions of a sort officers seldom asked.

MITSCHER BECAME DEVOTED to Viccellio's pilots on his second day, April 2, when three of them went ship-hunting at Vella Lavella and made a spectacular kill. Viccellio had worked out a new trick for the P-38's, a method of skip-bombing without bombs:

"Use your belly tanks," he told them. "When you catch a

ship you won't hurt her much with guns. If you have enough gas to get back home, go down to a low level, skin a belly tank, and when it bangs into the ship, the wingman can set the gas afire. It'll work like a torch."

Tom Lanphier, Doug Canning and D. C. Goerke flew west on the mission, and on their way home Canning spotted a Japanese freighter moored close by the shore, almost hidden by overhanging trees. Lanphier and Canning dived to within fifty feet and dropped their tanks against the hull. Goerke came close behind and as the gasoline from the bursting tanks spread, set the surface of the water aflame with tracer bullets. The ship burned furiously. A PT boat skipper reported her still burning the next morning.

Mitscher was delighted with the ingenious feat and reported it to New Caledonia. Halsey replied: VERY NEAT USE OF HEAT. YOUR TREATMENT IS HARD TO BEAT. COMMANDER 3RD FLEET SENDS . . . CONGRATULATIONS ON BIGTIME HOTFOOT.

THE JAPANESE OPENED THEIR OPERATION on April 7 with the heaviest raid Guadalcanal had yet seen. Coast-watchers reported them first, four large waves heading for Cactus: the count was 67 Val dive bombers and 110 Zeroes. Mitscher's command sent 76 fighters up to meet them: Wild-cats and Lightnings, with a few Corsairs, Warhawks and Airacobras. The planes waited, turning slow orbits through occasional showers, evading thunderheads over Florida Island. Beneath them a cruiser task force, which had just fueled at Tulagi, hurried for the open sea—the *Honolulu, Helena, St. Louis* and some destroyers. Several transports, a PT boat tender, some tankers and other small craft were left in the harbor.

At 1400 the radar screens were almost solid with the pips of enemy planes, and Condition Red was sounded, soon changed to Condition Very Red, an innovation of Control. A cloud of Zeroes came in over Savo Island, and Mitscher's force went after them; Japanese planes began falling at once, but the battle boiled in and out of sight, through the squalls, in Tulagi Harbor, over Henderson Field, and far out at sea, so that it was impossible to follow. In the harbor, the tanker *Kanawha* was set afire and beached; nineteen of her men were killed. The New Zealand corvette *Moa* and the U.S.

get yamamoto

the quarry...

Here he poses at the London Naval Conference of 1934, where the stubborn Yamamoto broke the old formula of naval parity and set off the vast building program which led Japan to war.

Yamamoto as naval attaché in Washington in the 1920's, when he studied American strategy.

The dynamo of I Operation. With less than two weeks to live, the Admiral exhorts his carrier pilots to strike hard at American bases. A few days earlier he had said sadly: "When the war began, one of our fighter pilots was the equal of five Americans, but no more . . . things are not the same." In this Headquarters scene at Rabaul, New Britain, Vice Admiral Jinichi Kusaka, the area commander, is at Yamamoto's right.

Fated to launch a war he feared Japan would lose, Yamamoto conceived the daring blow at Pearl Harbor. To critics he said: "It is our only hope in a war with America." Plans were made where he later awaited news of the sneak attack, in his operations room aboard the flagship **Yamato.**

Rabaul. Yamamoto took off from here on his last flight. Lakunai airfield, from which he left, is on the peninsula in the central foreground. Takeoff time was 6 A.M., April 18, 1943.

The pilots of I Operation seldom flew from Rabaul without a salute from the erect Yamamoto, standing beside the airstrip, impeccable in dress whites, cheering them on against the enemy.

the hunters...

Lightnings at last! The first P-38's arrive in the Pacific, to be used a few weeks later in the longest and most spectacular interception of World War II. These planes, just off shipboard, are moving through Tontouta, New Caledonia, to an airfield.

Puzzled airmen uncrate and assemble two dozen P-39 fighters at their first air base, in the Fijis, directed by a civilian expert—almost the only man ashore who had ever seen a P-39.

Major Henry Viccellio, chief of the 70th Fighter Squadron, greets a high-ranking Navy visitor during early training on the Fiji Islands. At right is Commander Lyndon B. Johnson, a young congressman-in-uniform on an inspection tour for President Roosevelt.

Fighter Strip Number Two, Guadalcanal, home of Lightnings of the 70th and 339th Fighter Squadrons, a rough coral runway lying between a deep ravine and a field of coconut stumps.

Major John W. Mitchell, already an Army ace, was the man assigned to plan, lead and navigate one of the most demanding missions ever flown. In his P-38, "Mitch's Squitch," he directed and flew cover as his attack element ended Yamamoto's career. Mitchell is being decorated for heroism on Guadalcanal by General D. C. Strother of the 13th Air Force.

COLLECTION OF REX T. BARBER

The Lightning was everything to Army pilots on Guadalcanal: home, hearth, fireside and sometimes a laundry yard.

U.S. AIR FORCE

Left photo: Lieutenant Douglas Canning, a Nebraskan, had the keenest eyes among Army pilots on Guadalcanal. It was he who broke radio silence at 9:34 A.M. of April 18, 1943: "Bogeys eleven o'clock. High." **Center photo:** After three days and nights of hectic preparation and careful planning, these three men were left to bore in to attack the two bombers of the Yamamoto party: Thomas G. Lanphier, Jr., Besby Frank Holmes and Rex T. Barber. The only U.S. casualty of the mission was Ray Hine, who flew on Holmes' wing.

Souvenir of a destroyer kill. Rex Barber, standing at right, holds the remains of his damaged wing, which he sheared on the smokestack of an enemy destroyer as he delivered a fatal bomb. Other Guadalcanal Army pilots, from left: Joe Moore, Bob Petit, and (kneeling) Lanphier.

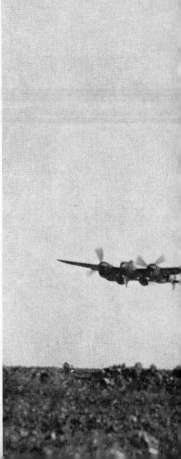

A mission begins. Drop tanks have been flown in from a distant base and installed by crewmen during the night. Just after dawn of April 18, 1943, P-38's of Major John Mitchell's 339th Squadron—loaded like these—rose from Guadalcanal's Fighter Two to begin their unique attack.

ambush at bougainville...

From the pilot's seat of his leading bomber, Admiral Yamamoto saw this landscape in his last moments. He flew southeastward between the mountains and the sea on Bougainville's coast, crossing Empress Augusta Bay as he neared his destination. Planes of American hunters, yet unseen, are slanting in from seaward, to the right; they intercepted Yamamoto a few miles ahead, above the jungle slopes in the upper right of this photograph. (The airstrip in the foreground was not then visible; it was built a few months later by invading Americans.)

Killer's-eye view of a Betty bomber. This gun camera, operated elsewhere in the Pacific, shot from almost precisely the angle used by Lanphier, Barber and Holmes in their two kills of the Yamamoto mission.

A pensive Major Mitchell, back home in the U.S., recalls the wild scramble over Bougainville as Tom Lanphier gestures to describe the dogfight for Air Force officers.

destroyer *Aaron Ward* were also lost, but the raiders did not sight the main task force.

The enemy paid dearly. Marine Lieutenant James Swett shot down seven Vals before he landed his badly damaged Wildcat in the water; Mitscher gave him the Navy Cross for the action.

Viccellio's men had a field day. As the planes scrambled, four of his veterans went up: Tom Lanphier, Rex Barber, Joe Moore and Jim McLanahan. They had waited with other Lightnings at 30,000 feet and dived on a formation of eleven Zeroes far below, working in pairs. They shot down seven of the enemy; Lanphier got three, Barber two, and Moore and McLanahan one each. Mitscher lost seven planes and one pilot, all Marines from Lieutenant Colonel Sam Moore's fighter group. It was the one raid against Guadalcanal in Yamamoto's new offensive.* On April 11 the enemy air fleet flew to the southwest, striking Oro Bay in New Guinea, and Cactus got an unexpected breathing spell.

MITSCHER LOOKED LIKE A SMALL-TOWN GROCER at work over his accounts in a back room, lost in concentration, gold-framed glasses far down on his nose, feet crossed atop the footlocker, his lap full of operational reports and messages from the radio dugout, lighting limp cigarettes in an unbroken chain, mopping his freckled skull and cleaning his fogged glasses with a handkerchief.

On Tuesday, April 14, a few hours after Admiral Nimitz had his morning intelligence briefing with Commander Layton at Pearl Harbor, Mitscher was handed a message from Halsey's headquarters in New Caledonia: Admiral Yamamoto was expected on Bougainville on Sunday. Only P-38's from Guadalcanal seemed to be capable of intercepting him. Would Mitscher study the matter and advise whether he

---

* The discrepancies between Japanese and U.S. reports of losses in this action were typical: The Japanese admitted to the loss of twenty-one planes; Americans estimated they had shot down thirty-nine. The U.S. said it lost seven planes, and the Japanese reported rather vaguely that ten defensive fighters had been "driven from the sky." Japanese claims of "most" of the twenty-six ships in harbor sunk were countered by the U.S. claim of only three vessels lost.

could shoot down the Japanese leader? The message was signed by Halsey's executive officer, Admiral T. S. Wilkinson.

Mitscher did not hesitate. He was confident that the Lightnings could reach Bougainville, just as they had strafed Kahili and Shortland earlier. Mitscher replied to Wilkinson, saying that his P-38's could perform the mission. The 339th Fighter Squadron, an Air Corps unit, would probably make the flight.

He turned to a chart and studied the large island of Bougainville, which lay to the northwest, some 320 miles away on a direct line. The island was marked with numerous red crosses denoting enemy fields and bases. Mitscher turned from the map as other reports came in, but his staff noted that he was edgy the rest of the day, his curiosity piqued by the message from Halsey's headquarters, and impatient to know more.

The Admiral called in several officers and began probing the problems of the mission, even before he got orders from Halsey. They talked of the route, the enemy coast-watchers on the intervening islands, the difficulty of navigation over open water, the range of the Lightnings, the probable defense of the visiting admiral that would be made by Japanese planes on Bougainville. Before he learned of Yamamoto's course, his time of arrival or the size of his party, Mitscher was convinced by his preliminary survey that only a meticulously planned, superbly flown mission could make an interception over so long a course. Among those he consulted were Viccellio and his successor, Colonel Ed Pugh, who agreed that only the P-38's could do the job. The logical leader of the strike, Viccellio said, was John Mitchell of the 339th.

The next morning a barrage of messages began arriving from New Caledonia. Halsey was back in his office, and the tone of dispatches became urgent. The mission had been approved by Pearl Harbor and Washington. Mitscher would begin preparations at once. During the day Halsey sent a copy of the dispatch which had been intercepted, decoded and translated at Pearl Harbor.

Mitscher read and reread the long message, making penciled notes of details:

> 0600 depart Rabaul . . . 0800 arrive Ballale. Depart immediately for Shortland by subchaser . . . arriving 0840. 0945 depart Shortland by subchaser, arriving Ballale 1030 . . . 1400 depart Buin by medium attack plane, arriving Rabaul

1540 . . . In the event of inclement weather, there will be a postponement of one day.

He hardly noticed that the order bore the signature of the Secretary of the Navy Frank Knox, or that President Roosevelt urged that the mission be given top priority. Mitscher put his staff to work. Officers divided the message and pored over its problems: was the "medium attack plane" of the message likely to be the swift new Betty type, or the older Sally? There was a discrepancy of twenty minutes in the flying times, on Yamamoto's flights from Rabaul to Bougainville and return; was this due to the difference in prevailing winds? Should the interception be planned earlier than the scheduled arrival, in the event of a windless day? How many fighters should make the sweep? Were there enough extra drop tanks to assure long range?

Mitscher's headquarters exchanged information with New Caledonia throughout the day, and requests for more intelligence went back along the chain to Pearl Harbor and to Washington. Late on April 15, or early April 16, a message went to 5th Air Force headquarters at Port Moresby, in New Guinea, asking for an emergency delivery of all available drop tanks, including some of the large 310-gallon size.

Mitscher left details to the staff as planning went on, but he asked several officers, independently, to draw up plans for the mission.

Sam Moore first heard of the mission on Saturday, April 17, as he stood outside the command tent at Fighter Two, where Mitscher appeared, leaned against his jeep, told him that Yamamoto was expected, and gave him the times of arrival and departure as if from long memory. Moore groaned. It was just the kind of strike he wanted for his Corsairs, but their belly tanks had been removed as hazardous in combat by a timorous ground officer. Moore told Mitscher that only the Air Corps P-38's had the necessary range. Mitscher nodded and climbed back into the jeep, muttering his soft profanity and complaining that the extra tanks had not yet arrived from Port Moresby, and that there could be no mission if they failed to arrive.

Sam Moore called his operations officer, Lieutenant John Condon, and they went to work; they had a plan ready in less than two hours, and Moore took it to Mitscher's headquarters.

Mitscher was soon back in his tent with General Harris and Commander Stan Ring of his staff. They were talking over details of the mission when Commander Gus Read, the operations officer, Administration, came in. The officers discussed the Yamamoto problem in a rambling way, moving from point to point. No one told Read that they were considering a top-secret matter. He listened with growing interest:

The pilots would have to remember the two-hour difference in Japanese and American time in the theater. Someone said that Yamamoto was scheduled to land in Ballale at ten o'clock; another said that the nearby fighter strip at Kahili would send planes up to greet the Admiral, and must be avoided. Major Aaron Tyer, the Air Corps commander at Fighter Two, came in and joined the conference.

The officers talked about the route the P-38's must fly, but only in general terms; they agreed that they must fly in an arc, to prevent sighting by enemy radar stations or coastwatchers on the islands lying between Guadalcanal and Bougainville. Mitscher turned to Read: "How's it look to you, Gus?"

"Suppose it's a planted message?" Read said. "How do we know they aren't sucking us into an ambush?"

Mitscher grinned. "That's been considered and discarded."

Read did not know that secret messages were involved, nor that the mission had been launched by code-breakers. The order directing the strike was not passed around. Someone said: "Why don't we plot the course he's likely to use down from Rabaul? Then we'll know what we're talking about."

Gus Read was handed a map and asked to mark Yamamoto's complete itinerary on it. He was not given a copy of the dispatch, but drew lines from Rabaul to Ballale and the nearby points as the itinerary was called off to him. When he saw the Yamamoto would make a boat trip of about five and one half miles from Shortland to Ballale, Read interrupted: "Why not shoot him down in Shortland Harbor, here about Faisi—that would take us far enough from Kahili. If they're planning an ambush, they'd never be waiting there."

Sam Moore had entered the tent, and disagreed: "We don't know what kinds of swimmers they are," he said. There was a brief debate over the point, but no decision was made. Someone asked, "How are we so sure he's going to keep schedule? Is he going to be on time?"

"You bet he will," Sam Moore said. "This is another black-shoe bastard. Those pilots will have him there on the dot." Moore offered the plan he had worked out with Condon, complete with a proposed course for the Lightnings. There was yet no decision as to how the interception should be made. Officers were still coming and going after two hours; the meeting moved into the dugout.*

They talked briefly about the Lightning pilots who should fly the mission. "Make sure you send Lanphier's bunch," Sam Moore said. "They've flown into Kahili, and strafed the hell out of Shortland harbor on one deal."

"Right," Mitscher said. "Don't leave Lanphier's element. I liked the way they scrubbed up the Japs last week. Let them pick all the rest, but use Lanphier and Barber and the other two. I forget who the others were."

"McLanahan and Joe Moore," Major Tyer said.

The conference lasted until late afternoon, beginning to degenerate into arguments over methods, before Mitscher said, "Let's get down to cases. Send for the Air Corps boys."

JOHN MITCHELL WAS LOAFING in the headquarters tent at Fighter Two, a couple of miles away, talking with Viccellio. The telephone rang. Viccellio answered and had a brief conversation.

"Mitch, go over to the Navy briefing bunker."

"What's it about?"

"They're cooking up something for your guys. Take Tom along and see what's up."

"What is it, Vic?"

"Some mission or other. You'll like it."

Mitchell and Lanphier rode over the rough coral road to Headquarters and went down into Mitscher's dugout. The dank room was full of men. A Marine major, a stranger, held

---

* The planning of this mission was so informal that officers who played major roles in the interception did not see each other. Sam Moore, for example, did not remember Viccellio, and for years was under the impression that the fighter chief had left the island by April 17, even though both men took part in planning the mission.

out a sheet from a teletype machine. "A little job for you, Mitchell," he said.

Lanphier looked over his shoulder, and both pilots glanced first to the signature. The message was signed "Knox."

Lanphier remembered the look of the blue tissue sheet for many years. "Top Secret" was stamped across the top. The text detailed the movements of Yamamoto and his staff on the visit to Bougainville. The order from Headquarters leapt out at him: SQUADRON 339 P-38 MUST AT ALL COST REACH AND DESTROY. PRESIDENT ATTACHES EXTREME IMPORTANCE THIS OPERATION.

The sheet trembled in the major's hand as the pilots read. Mitchell turned to Lanphier. "Who's Yamamoto?"

"Pearl Harbor . . ." Lanphier said.

A Navy officer took over, and the pilots became hangers-on in a council of war. "We found every brass hat on the island there," Lanphier remembered later.

"We're going to get this bird," the Navy man said. "If it took it, we'd throw in every man and every weapon on the island. We mean for you to nail him if you have to ram him in the air. But he'll be taking off more than six hundred and thirty-five miles away from here, and only good long-range flying will intercept him."

The excitement in the dugout was contagious.

The Navy officer talked of the need for a long overwater route, out of sight of land, which would add more than one hundred miles to the outward flight. They must also fly very low over the water, to avoid detection by radar. He peered over the heads of the crowd.

"Major Mitchell, that means Lightnings. We've got to have surprise at all costs, and nothing else flies that far and still gets there."

"Yes, sir," Mitchell said "We're ready to go."

It was almost the last word the pilots had in a debate that dragged on for another hour. Navy and Marine men offered theories. Lanphier recalled the scene: "Everyone pitched into the discussion. So many ideas were brought in that Mitchell and I were almost crowded out of the conversation. Officers of higher rank kept dropping in and interposing their suggestions for our conduct of the mission, until we wound up on the outer fringe of the milling crowd."

"Some of the ideas flying through the room got so farfetched that I began to fear for the longevity of those of us who had to execute them," Lanphier said. An officer on Mitscher's staff finally called a halt.

"Let's have Mitchell and Lanphier back up here," he said. "They're the guys who'll have to pull it off." The pilots shuffled through the crowd.

Commander Ring, Mitscher's operations officer, took over: "Major Mitchell, what do you say between these two plans —to strafe him on the subchaser, or kill him in the air?"

"I wouldn't know a subchaser from a sub," Mitchell said. "It'll have to be in the air. Nobody in our outfit is qualified to identify small craft."

Others interrupted. "But your guys did it last week," someone said. "How about that, Lanphier? Didn't you cream that destroyer?"

"It blew up," Lanphier said. "But Mitch is right. Our chances are better in the air."

"You'd never know if you got him on a ship," Mitchell said. "Hell, he could jump overboard or live through it on a raft—and you'd never really know if he had been aboard."

Ring told the pilots that extra gas tanks had been ordered from Port Moresby, and that they would be needed for a flight at wave-top flight, where the big engines would consume gas at an abnormal rate.

Other points were debated, and Mitchell and Lanphier were forgotten until Mitscher ended it: "All right, Mitchell's got to do the job, we've got to leave it to him. Is it in the air, Major?"

"Yes, sir. It's our only chance."

"Okay. Let's get on it."

Mitchell bent over Commander Read's map of Yamamoto's itinerary. "I'd say we ought to catch him here, west of Kahili, before he comes in to land."

"We'll leave the details to you," Ring said. "Is there anything you need from us?"

"Nothing but a good compass," Mitchell said. "I'd hate to trust my old Air Corps model on that close a run."

Ring laughed. "You'll get the Navy's best," he said. "We'll get it over tonight." He looked at his watch and the conference began to break up.

Sam Moore called to Mitchell, "If any of you guys get hurt, we don't want you submitted to interrogation."

The major grinned and drew a finger across his throat. "Don't worry," he said. "They won't lay a hand on us."

Mitchell and Lanphier emerged into the early darkness. They talked little on the jeep ride back, but as they neared the field, Mitchell said, "It looks like our first show together might be a big one. I want you to lead the shooters."

Okay," Lanphier said. "We'll give you all we've got. Give us a little cover and watch us go."

"Yeah. I'll get to work on it." Mitchell looked about in the cloudy sky. "I'll feel better if I ever see those extra drop tanks come in."

MITCHELL FORGOT SUPPER. He worked in his tent, alone at first, puzzling over his rudimentary maps of the Solomons area in the yellow light of a hanging lantern. He sat on the cot, plotting his course on a sheet of paper spread upon the blanket. Others appeared. Sam Moore had sent John Condon and an intelligence officer, Joe McGuigan, to help. McGuigan was soon busy with his slide rule.

The problem was obvious enough. The target lay almost precisely midway between Mitchell's base and Rabaul. Bougainville, an irregularly shaped island somewhat larger than Guadalcanal, was about 320 miles northwest of Henderson Field, by the most direct route. Since numerous islands lay between, most of them in enemy hands, Mitchell must fly a longer route, an arc over the open sea. Yamamoto would approach Bougainville from Rabaul in New Britain, a flight of about 315 miles.

"Let's start about due west, just south of the Russells," Mitchell said. "How far at sea would that take us from the nearest land?"

McGuigan laid his slide rule on the map. "If you shoot two hundred and sixty-five degrees, you'll have at least fifty miles clearance."

"All right. They'd never spot us out there."

"What speed should I figure?"

"Two hundred."

"Okay. This leg would run one hundred and eighty-three miles—that's fifty-five minutes."

"Then you could turn harder north," Condon said. "If they've got spotting boats out, they'd be between New Georgia and Vella Lavella, and you'd avoid them along this line."

"Right," Mitchell said. "They always have boats off the toe of Bougainville. Let's plot a swing to the south, and come in a little from the west."

"The second leg could be two hundred and ninety degrees." McGuigan said. "You'll have plenty of clearance past Rendova and Vella Lavella. Let's see—that's eighty-eight miles, and twenty-seven minutes."

They plotted a third heading, about northwest, 305 degrees, for 125 miles, flying time thirty-eight minutes.

Mitchell added the figures: "Okay, when we get that far, we'll be two hours out, and have flown about three hundred and ninety-six miles—that leaves us about forty miles offshore, just south of the island."

Viccellio came before they had finished and inspected the lines drawn on Mitchell's chart, with the estimates of flying time. "It looks like you've got it figured."

"Well, we're working out a guess," Mitchell said. "We've got to start with his arrival time. We want to cross the coast ten minutes before he's going to land. We figure him to land about nine forty-five."

"The message says ten o'clock," Viccellio said.

"Yeah, but the weather boys say there's likely to be no wind tomorrow, and if the Japs come down without a headwind, they'll be early. He has about three hundred and fifteen miles to come, and we estimate his speed at one hundred and eighty miles an hour. One thing we sure can't be is late."

"That sounds right," Viccellio said.

"I hope," Mitchell said. "They went over this thing with a fine-tooth comb at Headquarters, and that's their theory. Anyway, if he lands at nine forty-five, we want to meet him at nine thirty-five when his pilot is beginning to think about making the landing. If we fly at two hundred miles an hour, we'll take just about two hours to get to this spot, around forty miles off the coast."

"Are you going to bear straight in from there?" McGuigan said.

"Yeah," Mitchell said. "We ought to cut directly across his course. What's the heading there?"

"Twenty degrees," McGuigan said.

"Okay. We'll fly that. For the first five minutes, we'll stay right down on deck, and then we'll begin our climb. We ought to be getting up fairly high by the time we cross the coast, and if it all comes out right, we'll see him soon after we strike land. We'll leave the climbing time open, to see how it works out."

"Why do you figure he'll be coming down the eastern side of the island?" McGuigan said.

"If I were his pilot, and coming over water for a long stretch, I'd want to make landfall with him as soon as I could. They wouldn't take chances with him. But if he's not on the west coast, I'll fly straight across and look for him on the east. If he's not there, maybe we can shoot up the airfield."

"If your flight plan works," Viccellio said, "you'll strike the coast about nine thirty-five, is that right?"

"Yeah, and if he's doing one hundred and eighty and ahead of time like they say, that puts him about thirty to forty miles west of the airfield." Mitchell put a finger on the chart. "Right about here, just east of Empress Augusta Bay, at this little cup in the coastline. We ought to find that, if we can find anything. I figure nine thirty-five for crossing the coast, right there."

McGuigan left for Headquarters to make strip maps for the pilots, narrow charts six or eight inches wide and a foot long, each marked with the course. The mission's pilots would use them on their clipboards. "How many of these things do you want?" McGuigan said.

"They called for maximum effort," Mitchell said. "All we can manage is eighteen planes."

"Hell, I don't know if we can make 'em for everybody. Have you picked out all the guys?"

"That'll be no sweat. We've got the shooters, and nothing else matters a hell of a lot. The Navy wants Lanphier's gang."

Soon after McGuigan left, Mitchell shuffled through the maps on his cot and cursed: "How the hell do they expect anything to come of this?" I don't even have a chart that shows where the Japs are coming from. How do you like that? My map shows only our course. We don't even know from this where the bastard's been, or where he's headed."

"I suppose you want me to find someone else to jockey the show," Viccellio said.

Mitchell grinned. "In a pig's arse," he said. "This one is all mine. This is why I learned all the verse of 'Wild Blue Yonder.'" He went off in a jeep to Mitscher's headquarters

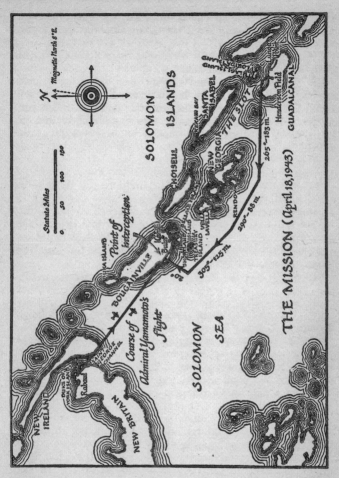

once more and copied details of the route from Rabaul to Bougainville from Commander Read's large-scale Navy hydrographic map.

On his way back Mitchell noted that the night had become darker and the air oppressively moist—the low clouds were heavy with the approach of Guadalcanal's nightly storm. Lightning flickered in the northwest, up the Slot, and a roll of thunder came in like naval gunfire. There had been no raid alarms. Lanphier's phonograph was blaring his worn recording of "Green Eyes"; it was one way to diagnose Tom's mood—the night before the outfit had heard nothing from his tent but the shouts and hoarse whispers of Maurice Evans in snatches from *Hamlet* and *Macbeth*.

Back in the tent, Mitchell completed his study of the flight plan quickly, and McGuigan brought him the strip maps. They were not alone for long. Rumors of the mission had spread through the command almost as soon as the Headquarters conference had ended. Mitchell looked up in astonishment as pilots crowded in.

"What's all this Yamamoto deal, Mitch? Put me down ... Don't leave me out, you Mississippi bastard ... When're we leaving, Mitch?"

They were still clamoring about Mitchell's tent when a severe storm broke; the pilots ran for cover in a driving rain. A few of them saw landing lights over the field and heard four bombers coming down for a landing on the long strip over at Henderson.

THE B-24's WERE FROM THE 90TH Bombardment Group of General George Kenney's 5th Air Force at Port Moresby. They swept in through the rain into the dim lights and thumped down as the storm neared its peak; before the savage lashing of rain ceased, a crew was hauling bulky gas tanks from the bombers, loading them on trucks and taking them to the fighters. Crews went to work in the revetments of Fighter Number Two.

The men threw tarpaulins over their welding trucks and the P-38's to shield lights and torches from the storm and from enemy planes, and the welders and fitters began their all-night chore, modifying the shackles which held the tanks. The rain ceased as suddenly as it had begun and the sky lightened.

MITCHELL ASSEMBLED HIS PILOTS on the hill above the strip just before midnight, but the crowd was so large that they moved the blackboard outside the briefing tent. He had pinned a list of eighteen names on the board, over the chalked scrawls of fighter tactics and the post-mortems of recent dogfights.

Mitchell looked out over the men, a hundred or more—forty of them pilots, all volunteers for the mission. The others were mechanics, Navy and Marine officers, reporters and strays from other outfits. The beam of his flashlight picked out the mission roster, and he called off the names:

"I wish I could take you all, but this is it: the attack group—the shooters—are Lanphier, Barber, McLanahan and Moore. I'll lead the cover flight: Jacobson, Holmes, Hine, Canning, Goerke, Kittle, Stratton, Whittaker, Graebner, Long, Anglin, Smith, Ames."

Mitchell snapped off his flashlight. "We're going after Admiral Yamamoto. We want him bad, but it's going to be flown as just another mission. It's all by guess and by God maybe he'll be there. Anyway, we've always wanted a real hell-raising fighter sweep to Bougainville, but nobody's ever been willing to risk so many planes on a strike before. Here it is. We've doped it out the best we can. The mechanics are fitting new drop tanks for us tonight. It's the same old drill: fly there by the flight plan, do the job, and come the hell on home."

Some of the pilots were strangers, and he talked for a time about flight discipline before he lit the flashlight once more. Louis Kittle had come to Mitchell a few minutes earlier to argue for the men of the 12th Squadron, and Mitchell had agreed; Kittle and seven of his men would fly in the rear of the cover group.

The beam of the flashlight reappeared and McGuigan passed the strip maps to men seated on the wet coral ridge. Mitchell began by calling off the course headings: "First leg, two hundred and sixty-five degrees for fifty-five minutes, one hundred and eighty-three miles ..." The pilots copied the figures on the backs of their maps, checking and rechecking them in the semi-darkness until Mitchell was content.

"Here's the pitch," the Major said. "We take off at seven ten, and will be formed up by seven twenty-five. This one's on split-second timing, so we can't have a screwup on the strip. We'll be about two hours and ten minutes on the flight out.

"Lanphier leads the killer flight, with Barber on his wing. We need at least four ships, to be sure, and if we have trouble, Holmes and Hine are the alternates. They'll join up with Lanphier's element if they're needed."

He roughed a map of the mission on the smeared blackboard. "Yamamoto's supposed to be coming to Bougainville tomorrow morning. We figure he'll land at nine forty-five. We're going to jump him there, to the west, ten minutes before that. They've got about a hundred Zeroes based on that field, and we ain't crazy to tangle with 'em.

"Our dope is that he'll be in a fast bomber, probably a Betty—and will have an escort of six Zeroes.

"We'll come in here, straight into the coast at about ninety degrees, and when we pick him up, Lanphier's gang will go after him."

"What altitude?" someone asked.

"Just a guess—about five thousand. Maybe even ten thousand. We figure he'll travel at under ten thousand to be comfortable and stay off oxygen, and by this time he'll be letting down to get ready for his run at the field.

"But whatever his altitude, this is the way we play it: Lanphier goes in, and the cover goes up top. We climb to twenty thousand, where we can see the airfield and cut off anything that gets in the way.

"No exceptions. There'll be no engagement by the cover unless they come up after us. Our job is to watch the killers and cover until the bombers go down. Nothing more. Okay?"

He briefed them for half an hour, swiftly and concisely. They were to fly at the lowest possible level, in complete radio silence, since surprise was essential. They would follow him on the headings, and he would signal each turn by a hand signal. The shackle releases of the new gas tanks would be explained the next morning before takeoff—about half the planes, including all those of the killer section, would carry big 310-gallon tanks, almost twice the size of those they had used on previous missions. Lanphier was impressed anew by Mitchell's confidence and intensity.

"I'll fly just like I know what I'm doing," Mitchell said, "and all you have to do is guide me. We'll go up and make our pass, and fly back at altitude, the usual direct route—the heading is one hundred and fifteen degrees. Hell, most of you could fly that in your sleep by now. It should take about an hour and an half to get back. If we get separated in the scrap, come home as best you can. Any questions?"

"How about the gas?"

"It may be close," Mitchell said. "By the book, our range is only six hundred miles at sea level using main tanks—and two thousand miles if we're at twenty thousand. They're putting drop tanks on all of us, but the big ones won't go around. If we get into a fight, some of us may have to ditch on the way home, but what the hell. That's the chance we always take. They're giving us the maximum range, but we can't kid around—we figure we've got only five or ten minutes in the target area, at best. Anything else?"

"Radio silence all the way?"

"Damned right. Until we spot him, or its clear we've missed him—or there's some real emergency, like an ambush. Don't worry about somebody spotting him, if we do cross his trail. Barber and Canning can see to hell and gone."

There were questions about the machine gun loads and the new gas tanks and survival kits, which Mitchell answered. As an afterthought he said, "I mean to tell you we'll be right down on the deck. Where nobody can spot us. But watch yourselves. If you drop just a few feet lower, you're in trouble. That drink will hypnotize you and you'll be in before you know it."

Mitchell stepped aside and McGuigan and Morrison took over.

"The weather guys say clear and hot," McGuigan said. Little cloud cover and practically no wind."

"How about the Jap ack-ack?"

"Plenty of it," Morrison said. He sketched the Kahili airfield and spotted gun emplacements from fresh intelligence reports. "You want to stay away from here if you can, but if they put up a bunch of Zeroes, you may be squeezed in. These are the trouble spots."

"Who says they'll have only six Zeroes?" a pilot said.

We're just going on the word that came down. You might run into slews of 'em. Remember when we had Knox down here?"

"How can you figure Yamamoto being on time like that?"

"Nobody guarantees it," Morrison said, "but we know he's

a stickler for punctuality. They all are, but especially Yamamoto. I've spent half of my life in Asia, and if I were betting, I'd say he'd be on time to the split second, barring a typhoon or an accident."

Mitchell did not notice what time it was when the briefing was over and he went to his tent. The pilots of the B-24's from Port Moresby kept him up a few minutes longer.

"What the hell are you guys going to do with all those big tanks we brought?"

"You ever hear of Admiral Yamamoto?" Mitchell said.

"Yeah, a little."

"Well, unless we screw up the deal, you won't hear much more. We're going after him." Mitchell explained the mission and the pilots whistled. "But on the other hand," Mitchell said, "it may be only a pipe dream. It's the wackiest mission I ever ran. You've got about as much chance of seeing Yamamoto, flying back to Moresby, as we have, considering all that could go wrong. When I stop to think about it, I know the damn thing will never work."

The light in Mitchell's tent went out immediately after the bomber pilots left, and he lay thinking of the mission: they could never meet Yamamoto across some 650 miles of open water, even if the enemy tried their best to keep the appointment; no pilot on earth could fly the course with absolute accuracy by dead reckoning, and an error of a degree or so on any heading could throw them off for miles and precious minutes; the air speed indicator, the tachometer, the compass, and his G.I. wristwatch were all fallible; even the slightest headwind could take him off course, and he would be unaware of it until too late; Yamamoto could be delayed, or wind conditions could vary between the two flights. Only madmen would expect such a long strike to succeed. Mitchell drowsed.

Glenn Miller's "Serenade in Blue" was playing from Canning's tent as Mitchell fell asleep.

The night passed without an enemy air raid, and around the fighter strip the crews worked, fitting the new tanks to the wings of the Lightnings, connecting fuel lines and testing controls of the improvised long-range system. The planes now carried auxiliary tanks under each wing, between the pilot's gondola and the engines. The welding torches had just sputtered out when dawn came abruptly to the island. The crews emerged from the tarpaulins into the cool air. The eighteen planes were ready.

8

Rendezvous at 9:34

THE PILOTS STRAGGLED INTO THE MESS TENT in the first moments of daylight, drawn by the odor of coffee. They went through the chow line with some of the crew chiefs, yawning and heavy-lidded, but came to life under the tent, where they battled clouds of early flies for their food. Breakfast was the inevitable offering: Spam and watery mounds of scrambled dried eggs, glasses of pallid blue powdered milk, and coffee.

The morning was fresh and the sky sparkled. As the weather section had promised, there was only the slightest breeze. The storm might have been a month ago.

There was little talk about the mission until Mitchell's high voice rose above the clatter. The Major continued to eat rapidly as he reassured two young pilots of the 12th Squadron opposite him at the rough table.

"Hell, all you've got to do is come right on the tail of the lead elements. And don't take that low altitude as a joke—your depth perception won't be worth a damn if you start gazing at that water."

To another he said, "I won't surprise you on the turns. Just keep an eye on your element leader. He'll pass back the signals."

Mitchell stood, chewing with full cheeks. He held a mug of coffee aloft as he stepped over the bench. His crew chief came to explain that the Navy had sent over one of the big compasses during the night, and that it had been fitted in his plane. "Thank God," Mitchell said. "Maybe we'll have a chance, now." He growled complaints about flying a long ocean hop by dead reckoning without a checkpoint, but he radiated confidence. He gave listening pilots the impression that the mission was routine. Mitchell left the tent and went downhill toward the fighter strip, balancing the thick coffee mug. "Don't be all day," he called. "We're taking off at seven ten, come hell or high water."

Breakfast and the flight line check seemed so normal and the day's prospects so unpromising, that even the pilots of the killer section, Lanphier and Barber, retained only one vivid memory of it in later years—Mitchell's rapid movement along the flight line, looking in at several revetments, speaking in his terse, smiling way with armorers, mechanics and crew chiefs.

Just before he climbed into his plane, Mitchell called to the pilots moving down the strip, "No replacements today. It's up to us. If Lanphier's guys have trouble, Holmes or Hine move up as shooters. Otherwise, no substitutes. And radio silence, damn it. That means silence."

Like most of them, Mitchell wore rawhide Marine boots, which would not come off in case of a parachute drop into the water. He clambered onto the wing of "Mitch's Squitch" and eased down on the dinghy seat, shoving aside the litter of emergency gear that was always there, including his "mad money," a bag of English sterling which might buy his way to freedom from natives if he were shot down.

The engines of the first four planes fired in unison, coughing oily dark smoke, then catching and throttling into a vast roar. Mitchell led them onto the strip. The planes had never been loaded so heavily, and they trundled near the very end of the runway, using flaps for extra lift, before they rose into the air. They zoomed over the coconut stumps, and Mitchell led them in a slow circle overhead, turning to allow the next planes to cut the arc and join him. Mitchell was followed by his wingman, Jacobson, then by Canning and Goerke.

Admiral Mitscher had come over to see them off and sat alone in his jeep on the apron of the strip, buffeted by the prop washes as he waved a hand to each plane, crinkling the seamed face with The Guadalcanal Smile.

The killer group was next: Lanphier, Barber, Jim McLanahan and Joe Moore, with Lanphier leading. He wore his usual clothes, G.I. pants, shirt and boots, and carried a sawed-off .38 revolver in a shoulder holster. Lanphier wondered wryly why he wore the pistol: "I couldn't hit a coconut

at six paces." Lanphier also had his customary precombat
stomach, a sour, uneasy feeling that disappeared as he rolled
the "Phoebe" into the storm of coral dust kicked up by
Mitchell's leading flight. He passed Barber's revetment and
saw the wingman in "Diablo," waving with a gap-toothed
grin, a reminder of his accident on Fiji. Lanphier's last
thought before takeoff was of Barber; he would be a good
man to have on the wing again today. Barber flew from the
strip close behind Lanphier. Joe Moore came next.

McLanahan bounced along behind them, but as he was
near takeoff his Lightning lurched off the runway, veering
wildly as the pilot fought for control; McLanahan had blown
a tire on a loose spike in the matting. There was no time to
wait for him. The killer flight was down to three planes.
Lanphier led them into the circling formation behind
Mitchell's first four.

The rest of the cover, ten planes in all, took off and joined
behind Mitchell's lead element. Holmes and Hine led the
way, with the planes from the 12th Squadron last, Louis
Kittle in the lead, followed by Gordon Whittaker, Roger
Ames, Lawrence Graebner, Everett Anglin, William E.
Smith, Eldon Stratton and Albert Long. They went into
formation, wheeling over the field and the rim of the bay.
Mitchell looked at his wristwatch. It was 7:25. The planes
had joined up in fifteen minutes, exactly as planned.

Mitchell led them in a gentle curve westward, steering the
first leg of his compass course, 265 degrees. They flew out
Sealark Channel past Cape Esperance, the western tip of
Guadalcanal, and were soon beyond sight of land.

The pilots switched to the new wing tanks as soon as they
were in formation, and only Joe Moore had trouble. His
engines sputtered as he switched back and forth, still unable
to start the flow from the new tanks, and caught the engines
once more from the internal tanks only by frantically working
the handle of his fuel pump. He pulled abreast of Lanphier
and made dejected gestures to indicate that he was getting
no fuel from the drop tanks. Lanphier motioned to him: *Turn
back. You'd never make it.* Moore grimaced and pulled his
plane out of formation and wheeled to the east. The killer
flight was down to two.

Lanphier left his place in the formation and flew up near
Mitchell, signaling that his section had been cut in half.
Mitchell turned and waved the alternates, Holmes and Hine,

to move forward. Lanphier went back into position with the new men following; he had never flown with them.

These changes had been made by the time they reached the Russell Islands, and the two leading elements were now in the fingertip formation planned for the mission:

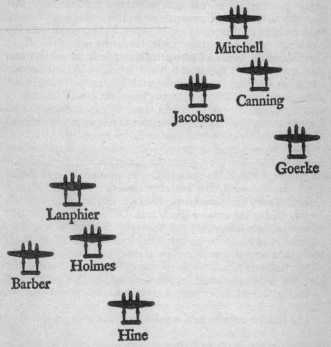

Mitchell

Canning

Jacobson

Goerke

Lanphier

Holmes

Barber

Hine

Kittle's eight planes were in similar formation to the rear—but though they formed up in this way, the elements strung out as they flew, to avoid the strain of close-formation flight. The planes were about one hundred feet apart as they settled down on their course. Mitchell could now see only the planes nearest him; the men of the 12th Squadron were out of sight in the rear. Mitchell set his power to give him an air speed of two hundred miles per hour. The thirty-two big engines hummed steadily. The swift shadows of the planes skimmed over the water, bearing almost due west. It was the anniversary of the first American strike against Japan—a year ago today, Jimmy Doolittle's raiders had flown off Marc Mitscher's *Hornet* to raid Tokyo.

BACK HOME IN THE UNITED STATES this morning, people turned to Sunday newspapers and saw the war stretching far ahead of them:

German armies, deep in Russia, held a huge bridgehead in the Caucasus; Soviet counterattacks made local gains. German armor struck the British and French in Tunisia, where the Allies held on. U.S. bombers hit a Focke-Wulf aircraft plant in Bremen, losing sixteen planes. The RAF, smashing Czechoslovakia's Skoda Works, lost fifty-five planes. The Japanese, dug in along the Aleutian Islands, were not budged by American air raids—thirteen on Kiska in one day.

The ten-cent Sunday *New York Times* listed best-selling books as *The Robe*, by Lloyd C. Douglas, and *Guadalcanal Diary*, by Richard Tregaskis. On Broadway, Milton Berle, Ilona Massey and Arthur Treacher starred in the *The Ziegfeld Follies*; Lunt and Fontanne in *The Pirate*; and Tallulah Bankhead in *The Skin of Our Teeth*. *Oklahoma!* was playing at the St. James Theatre.

Tom Harmon, the former Michigan All-American halfback, now a pilot, was safe after a crash in a South American jungle. Captain Clark Gable of the Air Force had arrived in England to teach aerial gunnery. President Roosevelt had spoken in Cincinnati, urging American women to aid the war effort.

The cost of the war had reached $7 billion a month.

THE LIGHTNINGS droned on monotonously. Mitchell tried to hold them at thirty feet, but they were sometimes as low as ten feet and as high as fifty. Mitchell once looked around and saw one of the planes lurch downward, too near the water; it was drenched with a froth of spray over the windscreen. As Mitchell watched helplessly, the pilot struggled, then eased upward to safety once more. The rising sun shone down on them, sixteen swift specks, fleeting alone across the vast, dark empty sea, trailing tiny white wakes as if they were a fleet of phantom boats; the wake disappeared quickly after their passage. The water raced beneath them at dizzying speed, so that the pilots were forced to look outward to see into the sunlit depths.

Canning noted that the sea was almost as still as a mill-pond, without whitecaps, and much clearer than the Atlantic. He spotted a huge shark, and when he saw another one, began counting; he would see forty-eight of the big fish on the flight, and one Manta ray, which he thought must have weighed a ton or more. Holmes, who had so often fished in the Pacific, saw even more—schools of sharks, so numerous that he did not think of counting them.

There was little else, no land, no ships, no other planes, no sign of the presence of man—there was not even a bird. Their horizon was very near, the edge of a cup rimmed by the easy swells of the indigo sea with only the metallic sky beyond. A hot spring Sunday morning, crystal-clear, with barely a breath of wind, matchless flying weather.

To their right, in the north, far beyond their view as they passed, lay Santa Isabel and the New Georgia group, Rendova and Kolombangara, islands where enemy coastwatchers waited with their radio phones.

Mitchell's watch showed eight o'clock. They had been flying thirty-five minutes—they should be about 116 miles out. Less than 300 miles to go.

AT THIS PRECISE MOMENT, nearly 500 miles to the northwest, Isoroku Yamamoto's plane rose from Rabaul's Lakunai airfield. It was 6 A.M. Japanese time. The Admiral was adhering to his schedule to the instant.

Yamamoto had been up early, preparing, as briskly as ever, for his journey. It was a clear spring morning and Rabaul was loud with birdsong. His aides had persuaded him to wear the less conspicuous khakis instead of his dress white uniform. American intelligence would go to any lengths to find him in this forward area, his officers said; the Admiral must change uniforms, for the good of the service and his own safety. The Admiral had only smiled, but when he emerged from his quarters his staff saw that he had made the concession and wore fatigues, but he had on his white gloves and carried a dress sword.

His chief of staff, Admiral Ugaki, who also wore khakis,

was startled by Yamamoto's changed appearance. He had
never seen the commander in fatigues, and he now seemed a
different man, lacking some of the air of dignity he wore as
the symbol of naval tradition. As they left headquarters,
Yamamoto and Ugaki met Rear Admirals Takata and Kitamura, the fleet medical and finance officers, who were to fly
with them today—both wearing dress whites. Ugaki saw that
the unintentional breach of protocol was embarrassing to the
staff officers, but it was too late for a change of uniforms;
they left their cars at the airfield and went to board the two
bombers, separating in such haste that Ugaki did not call
farewell to Yamamoto.

Admiral Kusaka was the last man to speak with Yamamoto
at Rabaul. As he neared the plane the commander paused
and handed Kusaka two scrolls and asked that he give them
to Admiral Samejima. The scrolls, in Yamamoto's accomplished calligraphy, were poems by the Emperor Meiji, one
of which was Yamamoto's last writing:

> It is a time for men
> Who were born in the land of warriors.
> It is time for them
> To make themselves known.

Samejima, who had sent out the fateful message on Yamamoto's itinerary, was to treasure the poem for the rest of his
life.

Three staff officers filed into the leading bomber with
Yamamoto: Takata and Commander Ishizaki, the Admiral's
secretary, and Commander Toibana, the staff officer for air.
All of the officers of Yamamoto's party were trained pilots.

With Ugaki in the second bomber were other important
officers: Commanders Imanaka of communications and Muroi
of the air staff and Lieutenant Unno, the fleet meteorology
officer.

The party left in two new Bettys of the 705th Bombardment Squadron flown by skilled veteran pilots, Warrant
Officers Hayashi and Takeo Kotani. Six Zeroes of the 309th
Fighter Squadron took off in elements of three immediately
after the bombers.

Several ranking officers saw the departure, among them
Kukada and one of his staff, Commander Masatake Okumiya,
who personally waved the two bombers off the starting line

this morning. Several officers watched glumly as the commander's bomber picked up speed: Admiral Joshima and General Imamura, uneasy over their failure to halt Yamamoto's flight, and Captain Watanabe, disappointed at being left behind.

The eight planes of the group swept through the faint smoky haze of the volcanoes, above anchored ships in the harbor and across Blanche Bay. They made the first landfall on a lighthouse tower on the tip of New Ireland Island.

Ugaki, who was in the second bomber, was traveling light this morning; in his pockets he had only his glasses, a handkerchief, cigarettes and his diary. He was the only witness who would leave a record of Yamamoto's last flight: "As soon as I entered the second bomber, both aircraft began their takeoff runs down the field ... we slid into formation and took a southeast course ... flying conditions were good. I could see our escort fighters weaving in their protective pattern; three remained high above and behind us ..."

The bombers flew, nearly touching wingtips, with Yamamoto's plane slightly ahead and to the right. They headed almost directly into the dazzling light of the sun, at an altitude of 5000 feet. Ugaki looked out to his commander's plane, which bore the number 323 on its rudder. He could clearly identify the men; Yamamoto had taken the pilot's seat.

The new Bettys were remarkable planes, with a range of almost 2300 miles. Only a few months earlier, when Americans met them west of the Gilbert Islands, far from the nearest Japanese base, they thought the bombers had flown from carriers. The Mitsubishi designers had sacrificed the Betty's armor for range, however, and it was vulnerable under fire; Japanese crews knew the ship as "Kamaki" or "Flying Cigar." Its two engines generated more than 3000 horsepower; cruising speed was 196 miles per hour, with a maximum of 272.

Ugaki relaxed, studying a chart of the area as a young crewman pointed out landmarks below and in the distance. The planes flew without incident over the open sea until they reached the western tip of Bougainville and followed its coastline southeastward. They had been in flight an hour and a half.

Yamamoto's party now descended to about 2200 feet and droned along the shore of Bougainville, whose overgrown lowlands were threaded with swamps and inlets, a drowned country of mangrove swamps and palms. To the north lay the Emperor Range, whose tallest peak, Mount Balbi, trailed smoke from its 10,000 foot cone.

The crew chief came through the aisle and passed a note to Ugaki. The pilot, Hayashi, had scrawled: "Our time of arrival at Ballale is 0745 hours." Ugaki glanced at his watch. It was exactly 7:30 (by American time, 9:30). They would be landing in fifteen minutes, about a quarter of an hour ahead of schedule. By 8:00 they would be out of the planes and on their way.

THE SUN ON THE BIG WINDOWS of the Lightning gondolas made them like overheated greenhouses, and the shirts of the pilots were already drenched with sweat. The fighters had been designed for high altitude and had no coolers; ventilation was poor. Mitchell thought that it must be ninety-five degrees in his cockpit.

Mitchell's eyes moved constantly, from his temperature gauge to his watch, to the water, to the altimeter, to the compass. Occasionally he glanced down to the clipboard on his knee, at the strip map on which he had drawn the course headings.

He made the first change of course at 8:20 by the G.I. wristwatch, pointing to the new direction before he turned, a wave that passed back through the elements. If Mitchell's calculations had been accurate, they had come 183 miles.

They flew the second leg in less than half an hour, and Mitchell turned on a third heading, toward the northwest. They were thirty-eight minutes on this heading, and by now should have passed Vella Lavella Island. They were two hours out, and had flown about 396 miles—only about forty miles to go. Mitchell then veered much more sharply, turning back to the northeast.

The pilots missed the radios; they had never flown so long without using them. They became uncomfortable in the close quarters. As Mitchell made this turn to twenty degrees, Lanphier was beginning to squirm; the long silence and the sun and his cramped position were oppressive. "All I had seen along the way were wave tops and the four planes of Mitchell's group ahead of me." D. C. Goerke had a gnawing feeling in the pit of his stomach; his fear that something would go wrong today was heightened by the nervous strain of holding his plane just above the water.

The new heading would take them directly to the western coast of Bougainville. They hugged the deck for the first five minutes of this leg, then followed "Mitch's Squitch" in a long, slow climb, a lift that became perceptible only when the riffled white wakes disappeared from the sea beneath them. The pilots test-fired their guns, creating brief rolls of thunder. Within less than ten minutes they might be in combat. Now the Lightnings closed up, returning to the tighter fingertip formation in which they had assembled at Guadalcanal.

Mitchell was thinking ahead to the landfall: What if he does come down the far side of the island? After I cross the beach I'll make one circle over the west side, and if he's not there, I'll cross to the east and circle again.

He pictured the scene at Kahili as Yamamoto approached, with every pilot standing by his plane, in formation. If they got word that the Admiral's party was being attacked, they would swarm up after them almost instantly.

The Lightnings were still under 1000 feet, slowly climbing. Lanphier's watch read 9:33, and he strained, looking westward into the empty sky. Long afterward he could recall that he had only one thought, two minutes from the scheduled rendezvous: Would the Admiral be on time?

The sky was clear above, and Mitchell thought that visibility must be almost unlimited. He should be able to see the mountains of Bougainville, even twenty miles away. I must be off course, he thought. At that moment the sixteen planes rose abruptly from the haze which lay like an enormous, invisible pool over the water. Mitchell was exhilarated: "All of a sudden it jumped up at me I saw Bougainville." A towering mountain range thrust above the jungle. He had hit Bougainville precisely as he had planned.

Beneath him Mitchell saw the small inlet just east of Empress Augusta Bay, like a color version of his strip map. There was no sign of life on the island or in the sky.

Lanphier looked about eagerly. To the right, on the horizon, was the blur of the Treasury Islands. He noticed that the sky was clear except for a cumulus cloud along the mountain crests.

Several pilots of the killer section had been here before.

Mitchell had often flown bomber escort here. Lanphier and Barber had sunk their Japanese destroyer off Fauro Island, and blasted the planes at Shortland, both just off the southwestern toe of Bougainville. They could almost see those spots now. The sixteen planes were in tight formation at 2000 feet, Mitchell's four, Lanphier's four, with Kittle's two sections in the rear. They flew toward the island on a course almost perpendicular to the beach. It was now 9:34.

Mitchell thought: Here we are one minute ahead of schedule. Where is he? He should be about three miles back to the west. The Major peered to his left but saw no planes. At that moment Canning broke radio silence. Doug's voice was low and steady, almost as if he feared the enemy would overhear him: "Bogeys eleven o'clock." There was a slight pause before Canning called again: "High."

Mitchell saw them against the mountains. He counted quickly: eight planes, two of them bombers. Two, he thought, and not one. Something's wrong. He glanced back toward the enemy. "Roger," he called to Canning. "I have 'em." He counted the six Zeroes again and was reassured; it must be Yamamoto—but could Lanphier's four planes take on both bombers? There was no way to know which plane carried the Admiral—but there they were, just where he had planned to jump them. Mitchell felt a surge of exultation. It was fantastic, but he had found the enemy right on target, only one minute off the scheduled interception.

Mitchell turned eastward, parallel to the course of the enemy, and began climbing. He saw the bombers as new and shiny, not camouflaged, just as if they were fresh from the factory. He was surprised to see how large the Bettys were. We've got him, Mitchell thought. He's brought lots of brass with him, and we'll get a bag full.

Canning had seen the enemy planes without surprise. They sparkled in the light, streaking against the background of the mountains. The Japanese were about three miles away, he estimated. Some of the planes were in showcase echelon, but at first he did not distinguish bombers from fighters.

His ears rang from the sound of his own voice on the radio; he would not recall, later, whether Mitchell replied to his warning in that moment of excitement. Canning thought only: There. There they are.

Other pilots in the leading sections also found the enemy immediately.

Lanphier looked to his left and slightly ahead, where he saw a few black specks several thousand feet above, and perhaps five miles away. They were like bursts of anti-aircraft fire, he thought. As he peered more intently, Lanphier counted two bombers and six Zeroes. Without taking his eyes from the enemy, he switched to his internal fuel and dropped his gas tanks.

Barber saw the Japanese just below the crest of the tallest mountains. He checked to see that his own formation was tight; he and Lanphier were close, with Holmes and Hine just behind. Barber also saw the Japanese glittering like silver, "bright and new-looking, eapecially the bombers."

Holmes saw the enemy planes as dark ships in mustard-colored camouflage paint. He was seized by excitement. As he wrote later, "I felt my hands getting clammy on the control column. My knees quivered slightly . . .What a time to get nervous, I thought!" Holmes couldn't believe that he was one of the four chosen to attack Yamamoto, and that the target was now in front of him.

Mitchell called to the squadron, "Everybody skin tanks."

Holmes replied, cursing, "I can't get the damned things loose." When he got no answer Holmes called Lanphier, "Hold it a second, Tom until I shake my tanks loose." Lanphier did not reply.

Mitchell shoved his throttle all the way in and turned upward to take the cover position. Jack Jacobson, flying his wing, began falling behind: "Mitch really poured it on when he began his climb, and I wasn't getting full power and dropped about 250 feet back. I tried to keep up, because I was supposed to cover him. And I sure didn't want to be left alone."

Mitchell was anxious to release his own tanks, but could not do so in the climb, and waited: I can't skin 'em in somebody's face, he thought.

Behind Mitchell and Jacobson, Doug Canning flew upward, thinking only of the enemy bombers: Why the hell don't we all go after 'em? But he followed in the steep climb.

On Canning's wing, D. C. Goerke tried to release his tanks but had trouble freeing them, and dropped behind; when they fell at last he gave his plane full power and caught up.

Louis Kittle's eight planes surged upward behind Mitchell's men, following the battle plan and heading for 20,000 feet. Lanphier's section was left alone below.

The radios were squawking with many calls. Mitchell barked to Lanphier, "All right, Tom. Go get him. He's your meat." The four planes of the killer group flew straight for the island, to cut the course of Yamamoto's party. A moment later, Holmes turned away from the attack and went westward, over the water, parallel to the beach. Holmes was now vulnerable, and Hine turned after him to fly his wing as Holmes struggled with the stubborn drop tanks, kicking and slewing his plane as he tried to shake them loose. The American killer group was again down to two: Tom Lanphier and Rex Barber.

The Japanese planes still moved serenely eastward, unsuspecting. Incredibly, they had not yet seen the Lightnings.

Lanphier and Barber were rocketing upward, fighting to come level with the bombers before they were spotted. Lanphier was nearly level with the enemy bombers, a mile to the east of them and perhaps two miles offshore, when he saw silver tanks flutter from beneath the Zeroes. They had been spotted at last. The Japanese fighters nosed down in a dive. The leading bomber winged over violently and the other swung toward the coast, directly toward Lanphier and Barber. Tom looked about. He and Rex were alone. Mitchell's twelve planes were out of sight above, flying cover. Holmes and Hine were nowhere to be seen.

Lanphier saw that the plunging Zeroes would reach him and Barber before they could close on the bombers, and he yanked back on his control column to bring his guns to bear on the lead Zero. He began firing long before he had pointed the nose in the enemy's direction. It was buck fever, Lanphier thought. "I wondered with stupid detachment if his bullets would start hitting me before I could get my guns up and into his face." The two fighters almost collided, but before the Zero hurtled past, Lanphier's cannon ripped one of the enemy's wings away, and he twisted out of sight beneath, trailing smoke and flame.

From above, Mitchell was calling Lanphier, unheeded in the din: "Leave the Zeroes, Tom. Bore in on the bombers. Get the bombers. Damn it all, the bombers!"

Mitchell could see little of the fight below; he did not realize that Holmes and Hine were out of it, and that only two Lightnings had gone after the bombers, to face the six escorting Zeroes. I should have sent more planes, he thought.

If only I'd known he'd bring two bombers. But then he thought: Hell, if we sent in too many they'd just shoot up each other.

9

Black Smoke
in the Jungle

SOMEONE IN YAMAMOTO'S PLANE, looking seaward, had seen them first—perhaps a tumbling gas tank or the dark silhouettes of Mitchell's cover force as it climbed, or the wink of sun on the propellers of the two killer planes, which were hurtling upward to cut off the bombers. The plane of the Commander in Chief plunged downward, seeking safety. It was the same spot where General Imamura had escaped enemy interception two months before.

In the second bomber, Admiral Ugaki looked up in alarm as the engines raced without warning. With the pilot's message still in his hand, Ugaki peered out the window. They were diving toward the jungle. When they leveled out they were no more than two hundred feet above the treetops. Yamamoto's ship had made a sharp turn to the left, fleeing toward Buin.

Ugaki's bomber filled with excited voices. "Nobody knew what had happened, and we scanned the sky anxiously for the enemy fighter planes we felt certain were diving to the attack."

The crew chief came back and crouched in the narrow aisle between the seats, but he could tell the officers nothing. "It looks as if we made a mistake, sir. We shouldn't have dived."

Ugaki saw one of the Zeroes dive near the bomber, the pilot pointing downward to the right. The crew chief shouted, "American planes!" The bomber pilots had dived instantly, without waiting for orders.

Ugaki heard the abrupt screaming of the wind as the

110

gunports opened, and then a metallic cranking, and knew that men were unlimbering the machine guns; the crewmen had finally come to their senses, and taken battle positions. Now Ugaki saw the Zeroes twisting in the sky, fighting the enemy, which he saw were "the big Lockheed P-38's," at least twenty-four of them, he thought.

The bomber swung hard, in a ninety-degree turn, jarring Ugaki. He watched the crew chief lean forward and tap the pilot's shoulder: "They are closing in fast."

Ugaki's plane was separated from Yamamoto, and the chief of staff lost sight of the lead bomber for a few seconds.

REX BARBER HAD PULLED UP TO 2500 FEET when the Japanese bombers dived, and he shoved his control column forward, swooping downward, flying inland to cut across their course. He crossed the coastline as the bombers began their dives. He knew that he was moving in too fast for accurate gunnery. The Zeroes above were within 1000 feet when he saw Lanphier turn up into them. By the time Lanphier was among the Jap fighters, Barber was upon the bombers.

"I cut the throttle all the way back," Barber remembered later. "When I saw I was about to overshoot the bombers I winged up in a vertical bank, and for a second or so my wing blanked them out of sight."

When he came back to level, Barber found a bomber in front of him; he was almost on top of the Betty. The other bomber was out of sight. Barber was surprised to see only one, but he now thought only of the tail gunner ahead of him. He knew that he was in the wrong angle for attack. "I should have been in high angle, shooting on the curve of pursuit. I looked right up the muzzle of that twenty-millimeter cannon—but so far as I know, it never fired."

He was catching up with the Betty swiftly: "I began firing into him; the bomber was shuddering at each burst." The Betty's right engine began smoking. "I thought I had hit some cylinders, but she wasn't burning yet."

Barber raked the fire of his guns from the engine across the fuselage, and as he did so the top of the tail section and part of the rudder flew from the Betty. The bomber did a quarter snap to its left, "the kind of a stall that would come from the pilot being killed and involuntarily yanking back on the controls."

Barber was very near the treetops now. He hurtled over the bomber, which was losing speed rapidly. He never saw the plane again. After he roared past the wounded bomber Barber looked back. As he remembered it after the war, "I thought I saw debris rising from the jungle—but I saw no fire. I felt sure he was gone. Farther back, I saw smoke rising from the trees, maybe two miles behind me; later I thought this must have been Tom's Zero. These glances were very rapid." He suddenly saw three Zeroes coming in at him from his right. Barber skimmed as close to the jungle as he dared, his throttle rammed to the firewall. "I hunched under that armor plate, believe me."

Barber feared that he would be shot down before he could escape his vulnerable position: "I kicked the ship up and sideways a little, yo-yoing, over and over. The Japs had to keep fighting themselves away from the trees, too. I slowly started to climb, and they fell a little behind me."

Suddenly, two P-38's flashed down in a high-speed dive, scattering the Zeroes from Barber's tail. The Lightnings swept inland; he never knew who was flying them.

Barber banked toward the sea. Only a few seconds—fifteen to thirty, he estimated—had elapsed since Lanphier began his climb into the Zeroes. Barber made a sharp turn toward the coast.

WHEN HE FLEW UPWARD THROUGH THE ZEROES, briefly losing sight of the bombers, Lanphier climbed almost straight up, kicked his ship over on its back and looked below for the bomber that had dived inland. He saw the furious action in a flash: a swirl of planes, among them Barber's Lightning, fleeing the Zeroes, and the two Zeroes he had just overshot, wheeling around to come back at him. He saw more: ". . . I spotted a shadow moving across the treetops below. I focused on it and found it to be the elusive bomber I was seeking . . . skimming along the surface of the jungle headed once again for Kahili."

Lanphier dived on the bomber. He leveled out, just above the treetops, and sped toward the bomber, hoping for a point-blank shot. He suddenly realized that he was flying too fast, and would overshoot the Betty. He cut back the throttles, crossed his controls and went into a skid as a further brake to his speed.

"As I did so," Lanphier remembered, "the two Zeroes I had not spoken to as we passed by upstairs showed up again ... diving toward the bomber from an angle slightly off to my right ... obviously to try and get me before I got the bomber." It looked as if the three fighters and the bomber would collide.

Lanphier had no more than a glimpse of the Zeroes as they dove upon him, but the look of the bomber now before him was indelible in his memory: "It was dark all over, an olive green, darker than the trees, but it was burnished so that it glistened in the sun."

Lanphier was stubbornly determined to make the most of his shot at the bomber: "I was no gunner, but I did know enough to fly behind a guy and spray him."

He fired a long burst across the Betty's line of flight from nearly right angles: "Long before I considered myself in range, the bomber's right engine, and then his right wing, began to burn ... The two onrushing Zeroes shot over my head just then." Lanphier saw the cannon in the Betty's tail open fire—but just as he came into its range, "the bomber's right wing came off and it plunged into the jungle and exploded."

As he winged over the treetops, only ten feet above the jungle, Lanphier saw that his speed was down to 220 miles per hour. Zeroes were on either side of him. Lanphier used his radio for the first time that day; "Mitch, can you see me?"

Mitchell looked down from above but could see nothing of Lanphier: "Where are you?"

"Hell, I don't know, but I've got Zeroes. I'm heading east, over jungle."

Mitchell could not find him.

Lanphier called again, "I got a bomber. Verify him for me, Mitch. He's burning."

Mitchell called to say he saw the fire. As he later recalled it, "I saw a column of smoke rising from the jungle, a big fire."

Lanphier escaped the Zeroes by turning into each one as it dived upon him; when they changed tactics, to come at him from opposite directions, the Zeroes had lost speed, and the

Lightning was gaining. He slewed and twisted the P-38 to escape enemy fire. "I hugged the earth and kept heading for home, ducking in and out of every little gully I came upon." At last he emerged from a valley at high speed, into a dust cloud; he had cut across an edge of Kahili air base. He roared over the harbor, and once in his highspeed climb, outdistanced the two pursuing Zeroes. When he reached 200,000 feet, Lanphier was alone. He turned toward home.

THOUGH THE AMERICAN PILOTS would not realize it until years afterward, only one Japanese bomber had fallen into the jungle, carrying Yamamoto, his staff officers and the Betty's crew to death. Lanphier and Barber alone had fought their way through the confusion, each to retain vivid lifelong memories of their separate attacks—perhaps, Barber thought later, attacks upon the same bomber. Each man was positive he had shot down a Betty over the jungle. The crash of the first bomber had come very swiftly in the wild battle above the island. The second was soon to follow.

ADMIRAL UGAKI'S STRICKEN FACE peered from the window of the second bomber during the hectic evasive action, until at last he spotted his commander's plane: "I was horrified to see the airplane flying slowly above the jungle, headed to the south, with bright orange flames rapidly enveloping the wings and fuselage." It had been no more than twenty seconds since Yamamoto's plane had made its first abrupt turn inland, toward Buin.

Ugaki saw the burning Betty about a mile away, trailing black smoke, dropping lower and lower. Yamamoto was undoubtedly still in the pilot's seat.

Ugaki tried to cry out to Commander Muroi, who was standing behind him, but was so shaken that he was unable to speak. Instead, he reached for Muroi: "I grasped him by the shoulder and pulled him to the window, pointing to the Admiral's burning plane. I caught a last glimpse myself, an eternal farewell to this beloved officer." Ugaki's plane swung over in a steep turn.

Tracers flashed past the wings, and the plane weaved back

and forth violently as Pilot Hayashi tried to evade the fire of a pursuing Lightning. Ugaki sat calmly through this: "I waited impatiently for the airplane to return to horizontal position, so that I could observe the Admiral's bomber." He hoped against hope, but he knew that the lead bomber would be gone. "As our own plane snapped out of its turn, I scanned the jungle. Yamamoto's plane was no longer in sight. Black smoke boiled from the dense jungle into the air. Alas! It was hopeless now!"

While Ugaki stared back at the column of smoke above the jungle, his plane straightened course and raced in the direction of Moila Point. As the plane crossed the coast and headed over water, Ugaki glanced behind once more; several fighters were locked in dogfights near the spot where Yamamoto's plane had gone down.

Two American fighters had now turned in the direction of Ugaki's plane.

WHEN BESBY HOLMES TURNED WESTWARD along the coast, still over the water, he saw Lanphier begin to engage the Zeroes, but very briefly. Holmes continued to fight his stubborn tanks, snapping the release several times without success. Ray Hine clung closely behind him, still protecting his wing. When the slewing of the plane did not free the tanks, Holmes dove sharply until his airspeed reached 350. "Then I hauled back on the controls and at the same time kicked the left rudder hard. Strong G-forces ripped the tanks off." The plane was clean.

Holmes turned to look for a fight. He saw many planes streaking through the sky. It was impossible for him to tell what turn the battle was taking. There was a babble on the radio.

He heard Rex Barber shout, "I got one of the sons of bitches! His tail fell off!" Holmes saw a bomber drop into the jungle and explode "with a terrific flash . . . a tight ball of fire, as though it had gone almost straight in." This was Yamamoto's bomber but Holmes had only the briefest of glimpses of its fate in the dogfight.

Holmes looked below and saw a P-38 just above the ocean, almost on the tail of a second Japanese bomber; three Zeroes were chasing them. It was not until afterward that Holmes determined that the pilot he saw below was Rex Barber. Holmes and Hine dived to the rescue.

Holmes recorded the next few seconds in his postwar memoirs: "I told Hine to take the Zero on Barber's right, and I slid over to get the two crowding him from the left . . . I let the first Zero have a long burst in his tail. I was firing straight ahead, without deflection, the range about 400 yards. The little Japanese fighter . . . exploded . . ."

Holmes claimed a second Zero: "I touched my triggers and watched the bullets nibble at the Zero's tail. The airplane fell into the sea."

By now, Holmes saw that he was moving at 425 miles per hour, much faster than the Lightning's red-line speed. He zoomed past Barber's plane. The bomber's gunners were shooting at Holmes. He fired a short burst to get his range, then another; his bullets kicked up the water behind the bomber, but he held the Betty in his sight.

As Holmes later described the kill of this bomber, "I touched the trigger. The fifties chattered and vibrated, shaking the whole airplane. Bullets tore into the Betty . . . I pressed the button to fire my 20 mm. cannon and listened to the dull POM-POM-POM of the shells as they exploded. It was the longest burst I had ever fired. . ." The Japanese gunners no longer returned fire. Holmes saw that he was more than ten miles from the Kahili airfield, where dust clouds were boiling up as about thirty Zeroes scrambled into the sky. He had little time.

Flying in extremely close, he lined his sight on the bomber's right engine and opened fire. The bomber would not go down. He followed on its tail, still shooting, until he was in danger of ramming the Betty. Holmes jammed his controls forward and dived beneath the enemy plane: "I saw the shadow of the bomber over me, and immediately hauled back sharply on the controls to keep from crashing into the water."

Then, as Holmes pulled up to make another pass, he saw the Betty crash: "The whole aft section flew apart from the bomber, about two-thirds of the way back of the wings, and tumbled into the sea with terrific force, broke into pieces and scattered. Barber bored in and fired at the wreckage and his plane was struck by some of the debris. The spot was covered instantly by a blaze that swept over the surface of the ocean, an expanse of an acre or more. The Betty sank from sight."

REX BARBER HAD A VERY DIFFERENT VIEW of this swift action at sea. He had escaped his pursuing Zeroes and flew toward the shore, where he saw the second enemy bomber low over the water, chased by two P-38's. As Barber saw it:

"The Lightnings were flying much too close a formation for any accurate gunnery pattern; the wing man was too close to fire well. When I was about half a mile from them they made a first pass at the bomber. It was all like a picture. I could see every move clearly. The lead man sprayed the water with his guns, but as he came over the Betty he did manage to bring fire through it. I saw puffs of smoke and a little trail of smoke from the right nacelle. I knew the Jap pilot must have firewalled his engine, or that the P-38 had hit him in a vulnerable spot.

"Then the wing man cut loose and sprayed far ahead in the water—perhaps half a mile ahead of the Betty. I swung toward the bomber and got right in behind him. The two Lightnings never made a turn. They just kept going." Within three minutes of sighting this Betty, Barber estimated, he had come up on his tail—only a plane's length behind. The Betty was within ten feet of the surface, perhaps lower.

"I was quite close now," Barber said. "I fired one burst and the bomber disintegrated. I was going pretty fast. He flew all to pieces. I thought that the lead man's guns must have hit the tanks and filled his wings with gas fumes, because the ship exploded in my face.

"I saw the flash and the smoke, and before I could move a muscle I was through the debris. A big chunk of metal cut a gash in a wing and something banged the underside of my gondola. I could soon see that I had some damage to my inner cooler, because I began to lose power in my left engine, through the supercharger. But all I really knew then was that he was gone, blown apart and down in the water."

ADMIRAL UGAKI LOOKED BACK from the fleeing Betty in these brief seconds of terror: "I stared helplessly as a silver

H-shaped P-38 half-rolled in a screaming zoom, then turned steeply, and closed rapidly toward our plane. Our gunners were firing desperately at the big enemy fighter, but to little avail."

Ugaki saw that the 7.7 machine guns of the Betty were not reaching the Lightning, which came in swiftly, and opened fire while still beyond range of the bomber's machine guns.

"I watched the P-38's nose seem to burst into twinkling flame, and suddenly the bomber shook from the impact . . ."

The Admiral realized that the American was firing cannon shells as well as machine gun bullets.

"The P-38 pilot was an excellent gunner, for his first fusillade . . . crashed into the right side of the airplane, then into the left. The drumming sounds vibrated through the airplane, which rocked from the impact . . . We knew we were now completely helpless, and waited for our end to come."

The Lightning clung tenaciously to the bomber's tail, still firing. One by one, the Betty's machine guns fell silent. Ugaki no longer looked to the rear.

The crew chief, in the midst of shouting orders to his men, choked, fell and dissapeared. The plane was a shambles. The Admiral saw that several of the crew were already dead.

Commander Muroi sprawled across a chair and a small table, arms spread before him. As the plane shuddered, Ugaki watched Muroi in horror, "his head rolling lifelessly back and forth."

"Another cannon shell suddenly tore open the right wing. The chief pilot, directly in front of me, pushed the control column forward. Our only chance of survival was to make a crash landing in the sea."

Ugaki could not see it, but a thick trail of smoke came from the right engine—it was to be reported later by a Zero pilot who had been flying above. When the Betty was very near the water, Pilot Hayashi pulled back on his controls in an effort to wrench it out of its dive. But, Ugaki wrote, "he could no longer control the aircraft."

Hayashi killed his power, but it was too late. "At full speed the bomber smashed into the water; the left wing crumpled and the Betty rolled sharply over to the left."

The wrecked bomber was alone in the sea; the American planes were high above, now fighting Zeroes.

WHEN BESBY HOLMES PULLED AWAY from the downed
Betty, he tried to call Barber and Hine, but got no reply; he
thought his radio must be out. He then saw two Lightnings
nearby—Barber and Hine. The three of them flew toward
the open sea. "I sighed with relief," Holmes said. "We were
through the mission, had shot down both Bettys, I had two
Zeroes and Ray Hine had gotten another."

As they turned eastward, Holmes saw a Zero in the direction of Kahili, beginning a dive on Barber. He could not
warn Rex by radio, so Holmes began a high-speed loop and
rolled to fire at the Zero: "The enemy pilot saw me, broke
off the attack on Barber and also pulled straight up. I went
up after him, throttling hard to get all the power she had."

Holmes continued to fire, though his right engine suddenly
failed and he began losing speed. His cannon ran out of
ammunition, but he shot the Zero with his few remaining
rounds of machine gun bullets. When he leveled his plane,
Hine and Barber were out of sight, and Holmes was alone
with his limping plane. He had seen nothing of the other two
P-38's since the Zeroes had dived. "My airspeed was so low
that I hardly dared take a deep breath." Holmes checked his
fuel gauges and saw that the right wing tank was empty. He
switched to another tank and the engine surged back to life.
Then he saw the cord to his earphones hanging loose,
plugged it in, and used his radio once more. He heard Mitchell's incisive voice, assembling the planes for the return flight.
Holmes turned toward Guadalcanal, alone.

BARBER REMEMBERED this action more briefly: "After
the Betty went down in the sea, I pulled up to get some altitude. A Zero came toward me and Holmes came back and
knocked him off, though the Zero wasn't shooting at me
then. I saw Hine smoking about that time.

"Another Zero came under me and rolled and I shot him
down. Hine disappeared. I could not locate him, nor spot a
place he could have crashed." Barber looked for a telltale
circle of bubbles, which were usually visible for miles. He
saw nothing—but Ray Hine was gone.

Barber flew back eastward, unable to reach high speed
because of the damage to his supercharger.

MITCHELL STUDIED THE SCENE BELOW ANXIOUSLY, and saw the dust clouds near Kahili. They'll be up after us any minute, he thought. He wondered why the Japanese fighters had reacted so slowly. He thought that the escort Zeroes must have no communication with the field: They'll be coming up now, anyway.

The chatter of his own pilots on the radio died as the dogfights broke up. He called to the planes of the mission, "Let's get the hell out and go home."

THE MEN IN THE COVER FLIGHT with Mitchell had seen almost nothing of the incredibly swift and furious action below. Jacobson said, "I saw two planes head for the bombers, then I lost track of what happened below. Things happened so fast, the sky full of Zeroes and Lightnings in a pretty small space. I saw something hit the trees and smoke, but I didn't know what it was."

The battle had been moving southeast down the coastline, Jacobson said. "The whole thing lasted about thirty seconds."

Roger Ames of the 12th Squadron could tell no details of the fighting below, not only because of the high altitude of the cover flight, but also because of "the amazing swiftness of it all."

Even with his sharp vision, Doug Canning saw little more. He climbed close behind Mitchell on the way up to the cover position, thinking with surprise that there were only six Zeroes. He had expected many more. If it had been American big brass, he thought, they would have surrounded him with escort planes.

Goerke had not seen the attacks below him, and at the end had noted only a pillar of smoke from the jungle—a downed plane, he thought, but he knew nothing of its identity.

When they reached altitude Canning was close behind Mitchell as they circled once, then plunged at high speed. He started down with Mitchell, keeping formation, but was diverted on the way: "I got on a Zero's tail, but my shield fogged. I had an optical gunsight and couldn't see a thing. Everything was obliterated. I tried frantically to wipe the shield by hand."

Canning was now about ten miles at sea. He could not find Goerke or anyone else. He went back to 18,000 feet, circling. He saw Zeroes taking off in dust at Kahili, but no P-38's. He thought the mission had left him, and flew toward home. By now Goerke had also seen Zeroes taking off. He fired into the dust clouds from long range, without a hit, then followed Canning to the east. He had not engaged the enemy, and no one had fired at him.

BY SOME MIRACLE three men still lived amid the wreckage of the disintegrated Betty in the sea off Moila Point. Admiral Ugaki, who had braced himself for an emergency landing, was numbed by pain or terror at the moment of impact: "I do not recall being injured in the crash," he wrote. He was hurled into the aisle from his seat, and his body was bruised and cut. He was stunned by the blow as the torn and wingless fuselage struck the water.

"I felt the crushing force of salt water pouring into the fuselage, and almost immediately we were below the surface. I was completely helpless."

The Admiral, convinced that he was about to die, said a requiem: "I vaguely recall that I felt as if life had come to its end; could not bring myself to move and could only lie perfectly still."

Ugaki did not lose consciousness. "I did not swallow any sea water. Everything was hazy, and I could not tell how much time passed ..." Somehow he escaped from the torn fuselage and lived through the roaring flame of aviation gas on the surface of the sea.

The Betty had fallen near the base at Buin, within sight of the field's control tower, and a rescue boat raced to the scene. A wounded man swam to the boat; he was the pilot, Warrant Officer Hayashi. "Take care of them," he said. Two others were in the water, weakly afloat—Vice Admiral Ugaki, and the Chief Paymaster, Rear Admiral Kitamura. They were the only survivors. More than twenty men had died in the two lost bombers and the three downed Zeroes. Ugaki was taken up tenderly; he had a broken arm and severe burns.

The rescue boat returned to land as swiftly as it had come,

and doctors were soon working over the rescued men in an air raid shelter. The last of the Zeroes descended to the field and quiet fell on the eastern tip of the island.

10

The Hunters
Return

IN THE LAST SECONDS OF THE BATTLE John Mitchell and Jack Jacobson circled over the eastern tip of Bougainville at 15,000 feet. They were pointing toward home when Mitchell saw a Lightning in trouble far below, smoking from an engine, with a Zero on its tail. Mitchell went into a dive, followed by Jacobson; they reached 400 miles an hour, until the planes were dangerously near buffeting. Mitchell fired on the Zero, which turned away, back toward the airfield at Kahili.

The major had a last glimpse of the crippled P-38 as it slid toward the water in a slow glide, still smoking from an engine. He did not see it strike the sea, and did not realize that the pilot was Ray Hine. A larger cloud of dust was now rising from the Kahili airfield, and enemy fighters were taking off. Mitchell and Jacobson put on power and flew toward Guadalcanal.

Tom Lanphier, who was out of sight, heard Mitchell and other pilots talking by radio about this time. Rex Barber's voice was excited, and he wanted more action despite his damaged plane: "I'm going to drop back and knock 'em off."

"No dice," Mitchell said. "Head back at once. We're under orders to evade further action—we've done the job."

Lanphier heard the brief argument which ended with Barber's reluctant surrender. There were a few whoops of triumph from other pilots over the success of the mission, but the radio soon fell silent. Lanphier settled on his homeward course. He had been shaken by the violent action; his hand trembled slightly and his teeth were on edge. Finally, slowly, he relaxed. His plane was undamaged so far as he could see. He had outrun the enemy and knew that he was safe: "No Zero in the Pacific was a match for the P-38 in a high-speed climb; the Japs knew it as well as I did."

Lanphier's only concern was the anti-aircraft fire from the bases at Kahili, Ballale and Shortland. A few black bursts flowered in the sky at his altitude, but did not come near his plane. He flew the most direct route home at high altitude, and was out of sight of his mates all the way home.

As he neared Guadalcanal, Lanphier saw that he was very low on gas; it would be a close call, but he had no choice. He had passed the Russell Islands, the nearest spot for an emergency landing. He went into a long glide, heading for Fighter Strip Number Two.

Other pilots had come in ahead of Lanphier; no one took note of the order of their arrival, but the first were men of Kittle's 12th Squadron who had flown with the cover, and had not been engaged.

Commander Read of Mitscher's staff first realized that Yamamoto had been downed when he saw some of these first arrivals doing barrel rolls over the fighter strip. It was then a little after 11 A.M. Within a matter of minutes most of the mission's survivors had returned.

Lanphier was the first of the killer section to land. Tom put down on the bumpy runway and was astonished to see his parking crew rush out to meet him. He quickly cut both propellers. The gas tanks of the "Phoebe" were empty. Only as he rolled to a stop did he realize how tired he was; it was the longest combat flight of his career.

The men who ran toward him were shouting and laughing—they were the familiar faces of his crew, with a mixture of strangers, mechanics, pilots, Marines and soldiers, charging the plane before he could clamber from the gondola. They swarmed about the plane and pulled him out, thumping him on the back. "I felt like a halfback who had just scored the winning touchdown."

Lanphier inspected his plane and found only two bullet holes in his horizontal stabilizer.

Rex Barber landed soon afterward, rolled to a halt and was surrounded by whooping crew chiefs and armorers. Barber's plane was badly shot up. The leading edge of one wing was deeply gashed and the ship was scarred in several places with green primer paint from a Japanese bomber's interior structure. Awed mechanics counted more than one hundred bullet holes in the "Diablo," six of them from machine gun bullets in the propellers.

Mitchell and Jacobson came in together. They had flown home at 10,000 feet, a routine flight. Years later, Mitchell recalled the moment of landing as a happy pandemonium: "Guys were coming in, piling out of planes, and we went up to each one as he came in. Some came to my plane and jumped up and down like it was a football game that we had won. All the crew chiefs turned out."

Jacobson remembered more: "Mitchell was jumping up and down; he was very excited."

Unnoticed in the crowd of celebrants was the lean young skipper of a Navy torpedo boat, briefly in port, who watched the welcoming of the heroes with an alert grin on his tanned face. He was John F. Kennedy of the PT-109.

Brief disagreement marred the return of the triumphant pilots. As Mitchell recalled it, Lanphier said over and over, "I got Yamamoto," throughout the hubbub, before anyone attempted a debriefing. There was an interruption when the intelligence officers, Bill Morrison and Joe McGuigan, pushed through the crowd to talk with Barber:

"How'd it go, Rex?" Morrison said.

"Great. I got two bombers and a Zero."

Barber remembered long afterward Lanphier's vehement protest, and a short heated argument over the bombers the two men had shot down. It ended amiably. "As long as we live, Rex," Lanphier said, "we'll never know which one of us got Yamamoto, and that's the way it ought to be."

Henry Viccellio was now on the strip, standing by as Morrison and McGuigan held an informal debriefing. There was little to be learned, except from Lanphier and Barber; they were the only men on the field who had taken part in the attack. They told vivid stories of shooting down their bombers, and of fighting off Zeroes. Lanphier and Barber agreed that each had shot down a bomber over the jungle. Mitchell confirmed that he had seen smoke over the trees when Lanphier called him to report a downed Betty. Barber told of shooting down his second Betty over the water, and showed the scars of his plane as proof that he had flown through the exploding fuselage.

"Okay," McGuigan said. "They must have added two Bettys after the message went out. We'll make it three bombers." Lanphier and Barber were each given credit for a bomber over the jungle, and Barber another for the bomber that fell into the sea; each was credited with a Zero. A final determination would be made when all pilots had returned with their reports.

Viccellio minimized the disagreements: "What the hell, the mission was a howling success. We didn't care who got the credit." No one was officially credited with shooting down Yamamoto.

The other pilots landed singly, each questioned briefly by the intelligence officer. The pilots of the cover force, including Mitchell, had little to report, since they had been far above the action, had seen almost nothing that happened below, and few of them had fired a shot.

Doug Canning was late coming home. When he climbed above the fighting and saw that he was alone, at least ten miles off the Bougainville coast, he had circled until he saw Zeroes coming up, then picked up speed to the east.

Near Shortland Island Goerke overtook Canning, and the two of them soon caught up with Frank Holmes, who was flying slowly. Canning came up on his wing and they talked by radio:

"I've got engine trouble," Holmes said. "Can you help me check my props?"

Canning put his plane into position and sighted through his own propeller until he could see that Holmes's was turning more slowly than his own. It was clear that Holmes had lost power.

Holmes was also low on fuel. He throttled back, using "just enough power to keep the old bird in the sky." He felt better with Canning on his wing, so that he could report his position if he dropped into the sea. Canning, Goerke and Holmes flew together toward home. Holmes was still switching tanks, trying to drain the last drops of gas, when he saw the Russell Islands below and went down for a landing.

Canning and Goerke watched Holmes put down safely and flew on to Guadalcanal. Canning landed about ten minutes after noon: he had been in the air about four hours and forty-five minutes. He was welcomed by a Marine who trotted down the runway beside him, and handed him a cold bottle of beer as he emerged. An intelligence officer came to Goerke's plane on the runway and interviewed him briefly.

Only when he had joined the other pilots in their victory celebration did Goerke learn that three bombers were reported downed.

HOLMES LANDED ON THE NEW FIELD in the Russells, scattering Marine steamrollers and tractors. He scrambled from the cockpit and did a war dance on the wing of his plane above gaping working crews.

"We got him!" Holmes yelled. "We got him!"

"Got who?"

"Yamamoto—the Admiral—the Pearl Harbor guy!"

Men crowded about him in an impromptu celebration.

"It was my island for a little while," Holmes remembered. The Marines gave him a gallon of water and called in a PT boat to refuel his plane.

Holmes tested his guns and found that he had only four rounds left in the machine guns; the cannon was empty. After a three-hour delay, he flew back to Guadalcanal.

Holmes returned to the field near midafternoon, the last of the pilots to come back, to find the others in the midst of an impromptu celebration. He got the impression that Lanphier and Barber were surprised to see him return, and were upset when he reported shooting down a bomber and three Zeroes. Years later Holmes recalled a brief passage of angry words over these credits, a memory not shared by Lanphier, Barber or Viccellio. There was a short argument over the "third" bomber, but the pilots left the haphazard debriefing without knowing who had been given credit for the kills. Viccellio thought Barber's version of the final attack on a bomber more convincing, but did not attempt to settle the matter. The pilots turned happily to their boisterous celebration.

Without further consultation with the pilots the intelligence officers, Morrison and McGuigan, gave Lanphier, Barber and Holmes credit for one bomber and one Zero each. After the interviews with returning pilots, Morrison and McGuigan prepared their first full report, which was to be completed three days later. Uncertainty as to which pilot had shot down Yamamoto traced to that document, the Combat Report of April 21 by COMAIRSOLS, which did not assign credit for the Admiral's bomber itself. The report said of the roles of Lanphier, Barber and Holmes:

When Lanphier and Barber were within one mile of contact, their attack was observed by the enemy. The bombers nosed down . . . the Zeros dropped their belly tanks and three peeled down, in a string, to intercept Lanphier. When he saw that he could not reach the bomber he turned up and into the enemy, exploding the first Zero, and firing into the others as they passed. By this time he had reached 6000 feet, so he nosed over, and went down to the tree tops after his escaping objective. He came into the bomber broadside—fired his bursts—a wing flew off and the plane went flaming to the earth.

The Zeros were now pursuing him and had the benefit of altitude. His mission accomplished, he hedgehopped the trees and made desperate maneuvers to escape . . .

Barber had gone in with Lanphier on the initial attack. He went for one of the bombers but its maneuvers caused him to overshoot a little. He whipped back, however, and although pursued by Zeros, caught the bomber and destroyed it. When he fired, the tail section flew off, the bomber turned over on its back and plummeted to earth . . .

Holmes noticed a stray bomber near Moila Point flying low over the water. He dove on it, his bursts setting it smoking in the left engine; Hine also shot at it and Barber polished it off with a burst in the fuselage. The bomber exploded, a piece of the plane flew off, cut through his left wing and knocked out his left inner cooler and other chunks left paint streaks on his wing—so close was his attack driven home.*

---

* Since there was no official credit for downing Yamamoto's plane at the time, no serious disagreement arose during the debriefing. The result was an imprecise documentary record of the mission's climax. As an Air Force officer who investigated wrote in 1967; "The Report is enough to make one weep. It reads like a fiction tale and the facts appear to be entwined like Medusa's locks."

It was not the purpose of this narrative to make a hypothetical case for either pilot; this account is based solely upon interviews with the pilots and the meager documentary record. There was some clarification with the publication of Zero in 1956, a book by Okumiya, Horikoshi and Caidin which revealed that only two Japanese bombers had been involved. The U.S. Air Force did not reassess the credits, and continues to award one bomber and one Zero each to Lanphier, Barber and Holmes for this mission. Air Force historians concede that this is not "a completely satisfactory answer."

Lanphier's later citation for his Navy Cross says that under attack by Lanphier "the leading bomber exploded in flames." Since

Irrespective of the report's uncertainty as to who had shot down the bomber over the water, credit for this kill was given to Holmes.

Despite the casual nature of the debriefing, Viccellio was content except for the loss of Hine. He questioned Mitchell and the pilots of the killer flight closely, but found that no one had seen Hine at the actual moment of his crash.

A few minutes after Holmes returned, Admiral Mitscher drove up to Viccellio's headquarters tent, grinning from the shadow of his baseball cap. As usual, he was alone—or almost. In the seat beside Mitscher, Viccellio saw an improbable treasure, probably a mirage, he thought: a case of fine bourbon whiskey, I. W. Harper. He had not seen a full bottle of bourbon since leaving the States.

Mitscher turned in the seat, swung his rawboned legs and thumped to the ground on his tiny scuffed brown aviator's shoes. He moved with unaccustomed speed, holding out his freckled hand to Viccellio and the fliers. "You raised hell with 'em, boys. They've been jabbering so much on the radio that we think you got him. I want you to know how good a job you did. By God, that's what I call flying!"

He pointed to the jeep. "I don't suppose you've got somebody who could take that case out of there?" Volunteers quickly had the princely gift in hand, and others ran for the

---

Yamamoto was in the leading bomber, Lanphier was officially credited with the kill of the Admiral by the War Department on September 11, 1945. Lanphier's articles on the mission were based on this army record crediting him with the kill.

Lanphier does not remember saying "I got Yamamoto," as Mitchell recalled (page 125). The dispute between Lanphier and Barber about Barber's claim of two bombers arose from the fact that Lanphier observed only two bombers in the flight and was sure of his own kill. The debate ended, Lanphier recalls, when Barber's second bomber claim was attributed to a third bomber not in Yamamoto's flight.

Rex Barber's view is that Lanphier, having zoomed upward to fight Zeroes, could not have identified the "leading bomber" when he returned to the pursuit—and that in the interim Barber's guns had already downed (or fatally damaged) one bomber. Barber believes that credit for Yamamoto's plane cannot be given with assurance—and that the War Department is either mistaken or that the two actually attacked the same bomber in rapid sequence. Lanphier is content to accept the record as it stands.

ice house, where they got ice and the only available chaser—grapefruit juice.

Mitscher questioned the men closely about Hine and directed Viccellio and Pugh to have patrol and rescue planes keep a sharp lookout for the lost pilot. "Perhaps he'll turn up," Mitscher said. "We've got to do all we can."

The wizened face tightened in a bitter scowl, as if he had thought of the fliers reported tortured by the enemy. "What you did today is worth as much as a big victory, men. That's the way we've got to win this war. It's the only way they understand. You can't trust the yellow bastards. In the end all we can do is to kill so many of 'em they can't remain a nation."

One man who was listening remembered what Mitscher had said not long before, about deer hunting. "Hell, I couldn't shoot one of the things—they've got such soulful eyes."

General Joe Collins also sent tribute from the Army—some steaks, bamboo shoots and beer, and the men of the mission had a gala lunch. Lanphier remembered the meal for a generation as his best of the war. The celebration went on until long after dark.

Back in the Headquarters dugout, Mitscher asked Read and Ring to draft a message on the Yamamoto mission to Admiral Halsey. Read suggested an opening sentence in the vein of the jocular slang effected by Halsey's officers to foil interception: "How about 'Pop goes the Weasel'?"

"That's good," Ring said, and composed the Admiral's victory dispatch:

> POP GOES THE WEASEL. P-38'S LED BY MAJOR JOHN W. MITCHELL USA VISITED KAHILI AREA ABOUT 0930. SHOT DOWN TWO BOMBERS ESCORTED BY ZEROS FLYING CLOSE FORMATION. ONE SHOT DOWN BELIEVED TO BE TEST FLIGHT. THREE ZEROS ADDED TO THE SCORE SUM TOTAL SIX. ONE P-38 FAILED RETURN.

Mitscher peered at the message through his glasses and nodded. He then scratched in an additional sentence to remind Halsey of the blow they had launched against Tokyo a year earlier: APRIL 18 SEEMS TO BE OUR DAY.

The message from Guadalcanal touched off an uproar in Halsey's headquarters at Noumea the next morning. At the daily conference, when Halsey read his officers the message and told them that Yamamoto was probably dead, the lean, dour Admiral Richmond Kelly Turner was transformed, whooping and dancing like an excited boy.

"Hold on, Kelly!" Halsey said. "What's so good about it? I'd hoped to lead that bastard up Pennsylvania Avenue in chains, with the rest of you kicking him where it would do the most good."

Halsey's exuberant reply had already reached Guadalcanal:

CONGRATULATIONS TO YOU AND MAJOR MITCHELL AND HIS HUNTERS—SOUNDS AS THOUGH ONE OF THE DUCKS IN THEIR BAG WAS A PEACOCK.

Halsey had second thoughts during the day, and sent two special orders to Guadalcanal: The mission was to be made secret, and no hint of it given to the press; the Japanese must not realize that their code had been broken. And two cases of "Combat Whiskey"—the best in the Navy's stock—were to go up to the pilots.

It was too late for Halsey's warning; by now many men around Headquarters knew that the Yamamoto mission had been flown, and that the Admiral had been shot down. Within a few hours men of John Mitchell's flight were herded out by a newsreel cameraman and posed in scenes which would never reach the American public. They rode up triumphantly in a jeep, posed before the war-worn planes, stood in a mock ceremony of decoration—and each man was interviewed at length.

By nightfall a fresh rumor was out: five of the participants in the strike would get the Congressional Medal of Honor—Mitchell, Lanphier, Barber Holmes and Hine.

ONE OF MITSCHER'S OFFICERS interrupted the celebration in the evening with an order for Viccellio: "The Admiral wants you to fly a mission up to Kahili tomorrow, without fail. He said he didn't want the Japs to get the idea there was anything funny about our striking today."

Viccellio looked about him at the veterans of the Yamamoto mission, still grappling sturdily with the supply of I. W.

Harper, and sent his aides elsewhere: "They'll be too far gone," he said. "Scrape me up about eight other pilots. I want men who know nothing about the mission, just in case . . ."

There was a bomber's moon that night, and Japanese raiders came early. Condition Red was sounded soon after sundown by a yeoman who banged a tire iron against an empty shell casing. The *Yank* magazine correspondent, Mack Morriss, who yet knew nothing about the Yamamoto mission, lay in his foxhole in a palm grove near Henderson Field, making notes in his diary by moonlight. He described four or five bomber passes overhead and some fires on Tulagi Island, just across the bay. He also heard the celebrants:

"This has been the noisiest raid I know, not so much from bombs and ack-ack but from officers who started singing early in the evening and are still out in the moonlight singing like a bunch of high school kids after a ball game."

Celebrating pilots brayed one of their beloved songs:

> I wanted wings and
> I got the goddam things—
> And now I don't want 'em any more!
> . . . I want my hand around a bottle
> And not a frigging throttle . . .

They sang an obscene chorus of "One-Ball Reilly" and stopped only when anti-aircraft fire came close. The songs became shouts of defiance. Men trying to sleep in foxholes and tents called insults: "Shut up, you goddamn USO soldiers!" Bombs fell occasionally at Tulagi, and tracers laced the sky. At 10:30 Morriss noted: "The songbirds are hushed." The all clear sounded soon after midnight, and Henderson Field and its outlying fighter strips returned to normal.

The eight substitute pilots were notified for duty at dawn, and Viccellio briefed them almost as carefully as if their mission were as important as yesterday's: "Don't make a fuss. But be sure the Japs see you. Fly the direct course, make one pass within plain sight of Kahili, and come on back. Keep altitude. Don't get into a scrap if you can possibly avoid it. Make it look routine."

In the first moments of daylight of April 19 eight Lightnings took off from Fighter Number Two—some of them bearing battle scars of the day before. They flew boldly up the island chain in the morning sunlight, over the mud flats and jungles where Japanese spotters waited.

11

The Admiral's
Last Voyage

NATIVES HAD GAZED IN WONDER from clearings in the Bougainville jungle as Japanese and American planes fought in their sky. The villagers of Ako, near the river Priaha, witnessed the violent end of Yamamoto and his men, which came in a yellow winking of American guns, a spattering of bullets in the jungle, shrieks of torn metal, explosions of engines, and the tumbling of the bomber's fuselage among the two-hundred-foot trees.

The Betty's remaining wing, snagged by the upper branches of trees, was ripped from the burning ship, which careened from trunk to trunk and fell to the forest floor. Explosions flung flaming debris for hundreds of feet. A greasy smoke pall rose above the gash in the green tangle, and through the smoke flew thousands of terrified parrots and cockatoos in gaudy flocks of scarlet, blue, yellow, green and white.

Soon after the planes had broken off the battle the Ako villagers conferred; some of them ran to peer at the smoking wreckage of the downed bomber, and a small black man from Ako trotted the downhill trail, carrying news of the lost plane to the Japanese.

On his way down the mountain the villager met a native road-building crew under guard of Japanese soldiers. He explained with emphatic gestures that a great plane had fallen near his village, and a young army officer, Lieutenant Tsuyoshi Hamasuna, abandoned the roadwork and marched his crew after the villager on the upward trail.

134

THREE ZERO PILOTS LANDED AT KAHILI in the surviving planes of the Yamamoto party, reported briefly and returned to Rabaul. Admiral Yamamoto's plane, they said, had fallen somewhere inland from the base, in the impenetrable hills. The second bomber was lost in the sea off Moila Point. The thirty-odd fighter pilots from Kahili airfield who had gone up to the rescue had seen nothing. They had been too late. By the time they reached altitude the Americans had fled and both bombers and three Zeroes of Yamamoto's cover had disappeared.

Smoke drifted over the burned bomber for almost three hours before 17th Army Headquarters at Buin recovered from the shock and organized a search. Headquarters had not learned of the discovery of the wreckage by the natives of Ako. Nine parties of soldiers and sailors were soon pushing into the jungle, among them a party of medical corpsmen.

Pilots from Buin began flying the slopes where men of the air base had seen a plane fall, but returned to their base at nightfall without having sighted the wrecked bomber.

A message was sent to Rabaul during the morning, before the surviving Zeroes had returned, but the stricken Captain Watanabe was delayed by a storm and could not fly to Bougainville until dawn of April 19. He took with him Admiral Okuva, the chief medical officer of the 8th Fleet.

From Rabaul, Vice Admiral Jinichi Kusaka, who delayed for several hours, hoping for better news, finally sent a coded message to the Minister of the Navy in Tokyo, saying that Yamamoto's burning bomber had fallen into the jungle and that the second bomber made "a forced landing in the sea." The message added that there were only two known survivors, Ugaki and Kitamura. (Pilot Hayashi was somehow overlooked.) The message ended: "The rescue forces are at work at present."

Watanabe arrived in Buin with his party from Rabaul at 8 A.M. and went immediately to the wounded Ugaki, who was lying in a dugout, his burned face swathed in bandages. Only the dark eyes of the Chief of Staff could be seen, and they brimmed with tears as Ugaki called hoarsely to Watanabe, "The Chief is there!" He pointed to the northwest. "There— only a few miles. Go quickly! Quickly, Captain!"

BY THIS TIME an Army pilot had found the scar in the jungle, winged slowly around it and reported; the plane lay upstream near the Priaha River, a dozen miles west of Buin. There was no sign of life, and fire seemed to have consumed even the wreckage. He could see little, for charred and torn trees leaned crazily above the site. The pilot was convinced that all aboard had been killed.

Captain Watanabe clung to his belief that Yamamoto was alive, and made bizarre preparations for a search of his own. He and the doctor flew to the spot in a seaplane, carrying many tennis balls which had been wrapped with a message: "Wave a handkerchief." The plane hovered over the jagged opening for an hour or more, turning lower and lower at Watanabe's insistence. The Captain dropped about fifteen tennis balls and watched them whisk among the jackstraws of the trees and disappear. Watanabe could not be sure that he saw the wreckage of the plane itself, and there was no sign of life; except for the mad ricocheting of the tennis balls, all was still. "Perhaps they are waving," Watanabe said, "but the jungle is too deep for them to be seen. Go lower." The distraught Captain wanted to jump into the jungle, but was dissuaded by the others, or thought better of it, and at last nodded to the pilot and they turned away. It was nearing sunset.

Watanabe joined the Navy's search for Yamamoto soon after he landed. His plane landed beside a patrol boat on the Bougainville coast, and Watanabe and the doctor boarded her, joining a party of sixty picked sailors. The small craft turned up the Priaha River, a swift dark stream that snaked through the jungle. The boat fought its way around the tortured coils until it was halted by the river shallows and barriers of fallen trees. The men divided into two parties and struggled upstream on the river banks for hours, stumbling in darkness, stung by clouds of mosquitoes, walking gingerly for fear they would stumble upon crocodiles. At daybreak they began hacking a trail into the rain forest, but some hours later, when the weary sailors had slashed their way only a couple of hundred yards from the river bank, a plane sent the party a radio message—Yamamoto's body had been found. Captain Watanabe and the sailors turned downstream toward their boat.

LIEUTENANT HAMASUNA had come to the seared clearing with the Ako villager, an opening about thirty yards square, deep in ashes, a tangle of burned trees and branches and scorched undergrowth. Amid this lay the wreckage of the bomber and the remains of eleven bodies.

The metal skin of the dismembered bomber was a sieve, pierced by numerous bullet holes, but the plane could be identified with ease; the tail bore the number 323.

Two bodies had been thrown clear of the fuselage before the final explosion. One of these lay across the remains of a torn and stained plane cushion. The officer had worn white gloves and his sword was in his hands. The features were so nearly intact that he should be recognizable; another, also obviously an officer, lay beside him, more badly burned.

The search party was driven into hiding for a few minutes by American planes which swept overhead, firing near the Kahili airfield; some of the excited workmen reported that bombs had fallen. The planes soon flew away; they were the Lightnings of the mission sent by Mitscher as a ruse. During the grisly work of recovering the bodies, Hamasuna was joined by two search teams from Buin, one of them the medical corpsmen. The medics examined the body of the first officer; he was still bleeding slightly from a chest wound; his sword was in his left hand. Nine other bodies were taken from the wrecked fuselage; the jungle's insect scavengers were already at work in the charred remains.

Hamasuna's natives hacked out bamboo poles to make stretchers and carried the bodies toward Buin. In midafternoon they heard the motor of the patrol boat on the Priaha, hailed her and took the burdens aboard. Watanabe and Admiral Okuva looked on sadly as sailors placed the row of bodies beneath improvised tents on the deck. They recognized the bodies of Yamamoto and Admiral Takata at once.

Okuva examined the body of Yamamoto and found a bullet wound at the base of the skull, ranging through the head and emerging at the cheekbone. "He must have been dead when the plane struck," the doctor said. "It was a mortal wound. A machine gun bullet."

Overcome by grief, Watanabe took the few personal effects from Yamamoto's body without touching the corpse. He removed bloodstained ribbons from his chest and insignia from his shoulders, his cap and sword and wallet. Watanabe found several poems in the wallet. There was also the Admiral's watch, which had stopped at 7:45.

The bodies were transferred to a submarine chaser and carried to Buin by sea. Sailors on the vessel speculated in rumors which would soon become legend: Yamamoto had crawled from the wreck, still alive, and had committed harakiri. Others said that Doctor Takata, in his last moments of consciousness, pulled the commander from the flames, placed his sword in his hands, and then died.

The story of the commander's end was taken to the injured Admiral Ugaki, who was overcome by a sense of guilt: "I am to be blamed for this incident." The description of the Admiral's pathetic end was almost too much for Ugaki. He was moved when he was told of Yamamoto's blackened body, still wearing tatters of his uniform, the symbolic sword still tightly clutched. "Even in death," Ugaki said, "dignity did not leave the great naval officer. To us, Isoroku Yamamoto virtually was a god."

Another search was conducted at sea. Navy divers were lowered near the spot where Admiral Ugaki's plane had fallen, and after an hour or more they discovered wreckage in the dimly lit waters, sixty-seven feet below. The divers found only the engines and propellers, wheels, machine guns, and an officer's sword. There were no bodies below—and no wreckage in which bodies might have been trapped. The plane had disintegrated. The bodies of two crewmen from Ugaki's bomber washed ashore on the morning of April 20.

Officers identified the bodies from Yamamoto's bomber by measuring their height and piecing together evidence from remains of their uniforms. The caskets were placed in the officers' quarters at Kahili airfield during the night, and a wake was observed.

Captain Watanabe led a funeral procession up a small mountain near Buin the next day. Workmen dug an improvised crematory on a green knob overlooking Buin and the sea, and men piled faggots on the coffins, poured gasoline over them and set off a leaping fire. An hour or so later Watanabe began the task of picking the bones of his old friend and commander, sifting the ashes from the dross.

He placed the ashes of Yamamoto's body in a small white wooden box which he had lined with leaves of papaya, the fruit of which the Admiral had been so fond. Sailors mounded the earth over the holes where the bodies had been burned and planted a young papaya tree on either side of Yamamoto's mound. A slab of native stone, carved with the Admiral's name, was placed between the papaya saplings. The party wound down the hillside with its eleven boxes of ashes.

ON APRIL 18 ADMIRAL KAKUDA, who had flown from Rabaul to rejoin the fleet at Truk, went aboard his carrier *Hiyo* with Commander Okumiya and others of his staff. As he stepped aboard, the ship's communications officer, obviously shaken, held out a telegram to the Admiral.

Okumiya watched his commander closely as he read the message. Color drained from the Admiral's face, and the younger officer sensed disaster: "Kaduda was a veteran combat naval air officer, known for his iron self-discipline under any circumstances. I was astonished to see the Admiral's face grow pale ... He uttered something unintelligible, and for some time afterward could not or would not speak to anyone. Admiral Isoroku Yamamoto was dead."

A solemn group of air officers joined Kakuda and Okumiya on the carrier's bridge, saluting the battleship *Musashi* as Yamamoto's flag was lowered from her mast. To Okumiya, the downward fluttering of the pennant was an omen of Japanese defeat: "... victory slips further and further from our grasp. Perhaps ... we who are carrying the fight to the enemy, as we are ordered to do, may still survive this conflict."

Word of the commander's death reached naval headquarters on April 20, but was known to very few officers, even those at Truk. Captain Watanabe, who had come down with fever, arrived at the big fleet base five days after the Admiral's death, escorting the ashes of the dead. The small caskets were placed in the commander's cabin of the *Musashi*.

Watanabe found in the Admiral's cabin some poems Yamamoto had written about six months earlier. The Captain was especially moved by one of these:

> So many are dead in the war,
> So many thousands of officers and soldiers,
> Loyal and brave,
> Who fought at the risk of their lives

And have now become a deity
Protecting the nation.

Oh, I cannot show my face to My Emperor,
Nor have I words to speak to the families
Of comrades who are gone.

My body is not iron or stone,
But with an iron will I will drive deep
Into the camp of the enemy
And will show the true blood of a Japanese man.

Wait for a little while, young soldiers.
Gloriously will I fight the farewell battle
And follow you
Some day soon.

THE SECRET WAS GUARDED as if the outcome of the war might hang in the balance. In Tokyo one of the few to learn of the tragedy was Admiral Mineichi Koga, Yamamoto's choice as his successor. The shocked Koga spoke for the Navy: "There was only one Yamamoto, and no one is able to replace him. His loss is an unsupportable blow to us." He also sounded a warning which seemed more ominous now that Yamamoto was gone: "Our enemy is striving for ultimate victory by expanding his preparations for offensive action and devising plans for the strategic application of new weapons." Koga appeared in Truk soon after his appointment on April 27, but the public was told only that he was making an inspection tour of the South Pacific. The Navy did not inform Yamamoto's family at this time.

IN BOTH TOKYO AND WASHINGTON it was felt that the course of the war had changed with the death of Yamamoto. As an audacious strategist he had no peer in the Imperial Navy, and no true successor. As the chief designer and builder of Japan's naval air arm in the years of peace, he had used carriers and their planes with an easy intimacy other senior officers could not match. Though the tide had begun to turn, and the growing strength of the U.S. Pacific Fleet would soon force Japan into a defensive role, Yamamoto could have been expected to strike as furiously as ever, so long as men and weapons remained to him. Under Koga and those who were to come after him, a more orthodox defensive strategy might be expected.

As an innovator, Yamamoto had won his place in history. His insistence on the development of the carrier and on such weapons as the aerial torpedo were proof of his vision. His use of massed carriers had revealed his tactical genius; the task force concept with which he had begun the war—and with which the United States was to end it—was evidence of his remarkable grasp of the realities of an air war at sea. Given the limited industrial resources of Japan, he had prepared the carrier Navy well for its war; his sweep across the western Pacific in the early months of the conflict was a notable feat in the history of naval warfare, involving planning and execution of a high order. What Yamatoto had seized for Japan in four months, the Allies would spend more than three years in recapturing. He had made errors, and he had glimpsed his failure before death—but there was not another such man in the Imperial Navy. The future had become darker for Japan in the few minutes over the Bougainville jungles.*

The Japanese people were told of the Admiral's death on May 21, the day the *Musashi* arrived in Tokyo Bay with his ashes. The radio announcement was brief:

"Admiral Yamamoto, while directing general strategy in the front line in April of this year, engaged in combat with the enemy and met gallant death in a war plane." There was no more: the announcer's voice choked with emotion, and he wept.

Two days later the fighting Navy bade its private farewell to Yamamoto on the *Musashi*'s deck, and afterward Captain Watanabe carried the ashes ashore, where a funeral train was waiting. Yamamoto's widow and four children met the captain on the train.

---

* There were other concerns for the Japanese naval command. Officers in Rabaul and Truk sent several insistent messages to Tokyo, suggesting that the Americans must have broken the code JN-25. The attack on Yamamoto, far away from enemy bases, could not have been a routine action. Tokyo's code experts insisted the machine code could not have been broken under any circumstances. It would be years before Japan's cryptologists learned of the American accomplishment.

Thousands of Japanese crowded the tracks to watch the slow passage of the train. Watanabe tired himself during the journey, holding the box of ashes up to a window, so that people might see it. When the train went into a tunnel shortly before reaching downtown Tokyo, an officer took the box from Watanabe and passed it to the widow and her children, who inspected it with calm reverence.

Yamamoto's ashes were divided and placed in two urns for seperate ceremonies, so that a state funeral could be held in Tokyo on June 5, the anniversary of the funeral of Yamamoto's hero, Admiral Togo. A second ceremony was to be held afterward in Nagaoka.*

The ashes remained with Mrs. Yamamoto and the children during most of the two-week interval before the state funeral. The oldest son, Yoshimasa, approached Yamamoto's old friend, Admiral Hori, in these days and said shyly, "I know very little about my father. Please tell me all about him."

Life in central Tokyo came to a halt during the state funeral. The official party was limited to 1500, but a throng estimated at one million packed the streets as the cortege passed. Only twelve other Japanese—and only one other commoner, Admiral Togo, the conqueror of the Russians— had been honored with state funerals. Except for the Emperor, who did not appear at funerals, virtually every Japanese dignitary in the home islands attended, including Prime Minister Tojo.

Services began in Hibiya Park in the heart of the city, near the Imperial Palace; some mourners noted that the geisha Chioko sat with a group of relatives and friends near Mrs. Yamamoto and her children. The young woman hid her face when press photographers attempted to take pictures. To the alien strains of Chopin's funeral march, mourn-

---

* Most accounts describe the division of the ashes into two urns, but Yamamoto's biographer Agawa wrote that there was a third parcel of ashes, delivered by retired Admiral Teikichi Hori to the geisha Chioko Kawai. According to this version, a separate funeral ceremony was held in a geisha house by Chioko and other friends, and Yamamoto's watch was also given to the geisha. Hori is said to have demanded that she deposit wartime letters from Yamamoto in the naval archives. This officer reportedly gave new hundred-yen notes to each of several geishas who had known Yamamoto well.

ers moved behind an artillery caisson on which the ashes were mounted, winding toward Tamabuchi Cemetery, where Yamamoto's urn was placed beside that of Togo.

Captain Watanabe had come from his hospital bed, weak and thin, but determined to take part in this farewell. He walked in the procession, carrying an open box containing Yamamoto's most recent medal. The captain grew faint. He staggered and fell and was taken from the procession.

The second urn of ashes was taken to Nagoaka by Yamamoto's seventy-eight-year-old sister, Mrs. Takahashi, and a final ceremony was held in the small town on June 7. Within the next week almost 700,000 people filed through the cemetery to stare at the urn, the uniform and sword of Yamamoto.

The ashes were buried beside those of the Admiral's father, the long-dead schoolteacher, in a small Buddhist temple on the outskirts of the town.

As Yamamoto had requested, his gravestone was humble, costing only about seventy-five yen, about ten cents. And as he had wished, the stone was cut exactly one inch shorter than his father's.

Epilogue

American

MITCHELL'S men had flown their last mission in the Pacific. Pete Mitscher grounded them immediately after the Yamamoto strike. There was gossip of a broken code, and speculation that they were being shipped for fear they would fall into Japanese hands; it was only now that the air command was becoming concerned over secrecy.

The pilots were flown out on April 23, ordered to Noumea, to the office of Major General M. F. Harmon, chief of Army Air Forces, South Pacific. Mitchell led them in—Lanphier, Barber, Jacobson and Holmes. Harmon and Doc Strother were waiting for them.

Harmon lectured them sternly: "You're lucky you're not getting court-martials. I never saw the Navy in such a lather. Damn it all, try and keep your mouths shut about this thing. From now on, you're deaf and dumb, and you're stateside."

The General then shook hands, smiling broadly. "You flew the greatest mission I ever heard of, and I'm going to give you the awards you deserve. I hope they're coming through with the Medal of Honor."

He turned to Mitchell: "How long have you been out here?"

"Seventeen months, sir."

The others had been out as long. "Hell's fire," Harmon said. "You fellows are going home."

"You can't let 'em go all at once," Strother said. "We need experienced men up here."

"You'll have to do without these," Harmon said. "They've had enough."

When the others left the room, Harmon told Mitchell, "If they don't give you the Congressional Medal, I will. I'm going to send you to General Arnold, and I want you to get

144

to Washington as soon as you can. He ought to know about this mission. I'll give you a letter."

When they flew toward home a few days later Mitchell carried a personal letter from Harmon to Arnold, full of praise for the fliers: "This was a beautifully conceived mission and executed from start to finish with high determination and consummate skill. All the officers participating are to be highly commended for this action. The Navy requested, and we acceded to their request to bestow decorations upon them."

Each pilot was promoted a grade as soon as he reached the U.S., and Mitchell, Lanphier, Barber and Holmes were awarded Navy Crosses for "extraordinary heroism. . . in the longest planned interception misson ever attempted." Ray Hine was awarded a Navy Cross posthumously.

Mitchell and Lanphier, who between them had shot down eleven Japanese planes, found themselves feted as heroes. They were sent on a tour of air bases to lecture young pilots on the P-38 and its capacity for meeting the Zero in battle. They were allowed to make no mention of the Yamamoto mission. At the end of the tour Mitchell and Lanphier were assigned to stateside duty for the duration of the war.

ON SEPTEMBER 11, 1943, almost five months after Yamamoto's death, Tom Lanphier's brother Charlie was shot down and captured as he led a flight of Marine Corsairs on a strafing raid at Kahili airfield. He parachuted safely to earth not far from the spot where Yamamoto had fallen, and was taken to prison near Rabaul. Fear of reprisal against him stiffened the Army's resolve to conceal Tom's role in the assassination.

Charlie died in camp two weeks before U. S. Marines liberated the prisoners at Rabaul.

MANY YEARS AFTERWARD, in 1949, when details of the Yamamoto misson had begun to recede in his memory, Tom Lanphier was startled by an unexpected reminder of the moments of furious action in the April skies over the jungle.

The Air Force Association, in celebration of Wright Brothers Week, hoped to beat the old record of five days for commercial airliner flight around the world, and sent Lanphier as its representative. Tom set a new mark of four days and some hours, but after his experience in Tokyo, hardly took note of the accomplishment.

His flight from Hong Kong to Tokyo landed after midnight, but as his plane stopped, Lanphier saw that a vast crowd was on hand, bathed in the floodlights and looking expectantly toward the ship. A Pan American agent came aboard to see Lanphier.

"Admiral Yamamoto's widow is waiting for you out there," he said. "She has come to greet you."

Lanphier was incredulous, but the agent was in earnest. "A Tokyo newspaper arranged it," he said. "This is their idea of improving international relations."

Lanphier emerged to find Mrs. Yamamoto at the foot of the ramp with an armful of flowers, a grave and matronly woman who spoke softly in Japanese to an interpreter, her eyes never leaving Lanphier's face There was no resentment or hatred in her expression, only amiability and a sort of yearning friendliness. Lanphier sensed the same feeling in the crowd.

As the interpreter relayed her words, she welcomed Lanphier to Japan, and held out her flowers to him. Her son, she said, was to be a student at Harvard.

The flustered Lanphier stumbled through an expression of appreciation for her coming to bid him welcome. They shook hands and parted, with the crowd still standing about them, as if reluctant to leave.

THERE WAS ANOTHER TRAGIC REMINDER of the Yamamoto mission for Tom Lanphier a few weeks later. The body of his brother Charlie was brought home from its grave near Rabaul and was buried with military honors at Arlington Cemetery. Tom stood at the graveside with his parents and his brother Jim: "I thought of how strangely my brother's life and mine had been linked with the remote island in the Solomons, and with a man neither of us ever saw: Admiral Isoroku Yamamoto." He recalled vividly as he stood in the cold rain at Arlington the green fiddle shape of Bougainville, a landscape he would never forget.*

Japanese

YAMAMOTO HAD FORECAST a year to eighteen months of Japanese victories after the destruction of the U.S. Pacific Fleet. It was one year, four months and eleven days after Pearl Harbor when he was killed, and after him there were no major Japanese victories; there were only growing disasters, coming ever nearer the home islands.

The Admiral's disciple and successor, Koga, died much as Yamamoto had died, in the crash of his plane off the Philippine coast in March, 1944. Despite reports that Koga's plane was the victim of a storm, there was a lurking suspicion that this officer, too, had been struck down in an American aerial ambush.

Admiral Matome Ugaki, the survivor of the Bougainville attack, died on the last day of the war, August 15, 1945, shortly after Hiroshima and Nagasaki were destroyed by atomic bombs. He was the leader of a Kamikaze mission against the vast American fleet at Okinawa. The commander of all Kamikaze planes on Kyushu, Ugaki was still thinking of Yamamoto when the war came to an end. In the morning he told an old friend, "This is my last chance to die like a warrior. I must be permitted that chance."

At noon of August 15, in a stunning break with tradition, Emperor Hirohito addressed the Japanese people by radio; Ugaki heard the thin, quavering voice in his headquarters, a

---

* After the war Lanphier led a distinguished career, as managing editor of the Idaho *Statesman*, special assistant to Air Force Secretary Stuart Symington, vice-president of Convair, president of Fairbanks-Morse, vice-president of Raytheon, and president of both the Air Force Association and the National Aeronautical Association. Other leading pilots of the mission spent many years in the Air Force. Barber and Mitchell retired in the late 1950's; Barber is now an insurance agent and rancher in Culver, Oregon, and Mitchell is a promoter of gas well properties in West Virginia. Holmes and Canning, both lieutenant colonels, were still in service in 1968, and Canning was an active pilot, flying cargo planes to Viet Nam. Viccellio, a lieutenant general, rose to command the Continental Air Command.

cave near Oita air base, far southwest of Tokyo. The Emperor announced the surrender of Japan. Millions of listeners sobbed hysterically, but Ugaki drank a ceremonial cup of sake, said goodbye to friends, stripped his uniform of its braid and insignia, and went from his cave toward his plane on the runway. One of his young officers, Captain Tamashi Miyazaki, trotted at his side, begging to be allowed to fly with him. The Admiral refused, ordering him to his duty. But when he reached his plane Ugaki was astounded to find ten fighter bombers ready for takeoff, with their crewmen standing rigidly alongside. "Are you so willing to die with me?" Ugaki asked. The young men raised their hands in salute, and Ugaki led them into the hot August sky.

About two hours later, when the flight should have been near Okinawa, Oita air base heard Ugaki's last words as his radio crackled a message to his planes: "I alone am to blame for our failure to defend the homeland and destroy the arrogant enemy. . . "

Ugaki and his flight dissappeared. The U.S. Navy reported no Kamikaze attack on the fleet that day, but the eleven planes did not return.

YAMAMOTO WAS NOT FORGOTTEN. Six months after his funeral, in December, 1943, a bronze statue of the Admiral was unveiled at the Kasumigaura Flying School, where he had once commanded, and where he had begun the long preparations for an air strike against the United States. The likeness of the manfully erect little Admiral survived bombing raids, even the fire storms which consumed many Japanese cities. In late 1945, when General MacArthur arrived to oversee the occupation of Japan, the bronze features of Yamamoto still gazed across the drill fields.

One of MacArthur's first orders banned monuments to war heroes, and statues were dismantled throughout Japan. Naval officers had Yamamoto's statue cut in two and hid it in a nearby lake, carefully mapping its location.

In 1955 a scrap dealer near Kasumigaura, dragging the lake for statues from which he could obtain precious copper, dredged up the bronze head and shoulders of Yamamoto. Several of the Admiral's wartime friends bought the statue and moved it to Nagaoka, where it was mounted on a stone pedestal in a park created by public subscription and named for Yamamoto. The statue stands beside a replica of the small wooden house in which Yamamoto was born, on the site of the original, which was lost in one of the last American fire raids.

Another memorial, seldom noticed by the city's throngs, marks the grave of Yamamoto's ashes in Tamabuchi Cemetery in Tokyo. Once each week an aging businessman visits the grave. He is the former Captain Yasuji Watanabe, now an employee of the American diesel firm, Cummins. His small automobile halts nearby and he goes reverently to the grave of his old chief, where he slowly dusts the polished stone with a silk handkerchief and then, after a few moments, disappears into the maelstrom of Tokyo traffic.

Acknowledgments

I AM GRATEFUL to participants of the Yamamoto mission whose recollections form the basis of this narrative: John W. Mitchell, San Anselmo, California; Thomas G. Lanphier, Jr., La Jolla, California; Rex T. Barber, Culver, Oregon; Lieutenant Colonel Douglas S. Canning USAF, Scott Air Force Base, Illinois; Jack Jacobson, San Diego, California; and to Besby F. Holmes and D. C. Goerke, of San Francisco.

Lieutenant General Henry Viccellio, USAF, who was squadron commander of most of these pilots, and Brigadier General D. C. Strother, who was chief of the 13th Fighter Command, also made major contributions, I am indebted to Vice Admiral William A. Read, USNR, Retired, and to Colonel Sam Moore, USMC, Retired, and to Mack Morriss, for their accounts of the development of the mission on Guadalcanal, and to Mrs. Marc A. Mitscher for information about her late husband.

For aid in reconstructing the story of the intercepted message of 13 April, 1943, I am grateful to Rear Admirals Edwin T. Layton and William C. Mott, USN, Retired; Captains Thomas H. Dyer and Wesley Wright and Charles N. Spinks, USN, Retired, and to Ladislas Farago and David Kahn, authors of recent works on American cryptography.

Basic documents on the American phase of the mission were located by the staff of the Aerospace Studies Institute, Maxwell Air Force Base, Alabama, and I am especially grateful to Miss Margot Kennedy, Dr. Albert F. Simpson and Dr. Maurer Maurer. Miss Bettie Sprigg of the Pentagon's Magazine and Book Branch was most helpful in locating photographs and other materials.

My very helpful translators of Japanese material were Dr. Chonghan Kim, Dr. Kee Choi and Dr. Terumi Tokita of the

College of William and Mary, Michihiro Miyagi of Ohio State University, and Mrs. John Toland of Danbury, Connecticut.

I am indebted to several Japanese correspondents who furnished previously unpublished information, especially to Yasuji Watanabe, once Yamamoto's aide; Eiichi Sorimachi, the Admiral's biographer; and to Colonel Susumu Nishiura, Director of War History, Japan Defense Agency.

Sergeant John Wible, USAF, who has devoted several years to research on the Yamamoto mission, gave helpful information and advice.

I must express my appreciation to those who read portions of the manuscript in its early stages: Admiral Chester W. Nimitz, Jr.; Admiral E. T. Layton; Captain Thomas H. Dyer, Colonel A. B. Lasswell; Colonels John W. Mitchell and Thomas G. Lanphier Jr.; and John Toland and Ladislas Farago.

Among the important printed sources was a brief article, "To Kill an Admiral," by Marshal Michel, in *Aerospace Historian*, Spring, 1966.

Among published books consulted, the following were most helpful:

The Human Side of Isoroku Yamamoto, Carrier Marshal, by Eiichi Sorimachi, Tokyo, 1955.

Isoroku Yamamoto, by Hiroyuki Agawa, Tokyo, 1965.

Yamamoto, by John Deane Potter, New York, 1965.

The Magnificent Mitscher, by Theodore Taylor, New York, 1954.

Zero, by Masatake Okumiya, Jiro Horikoshi and Martin Caidin, New York, 1956.

The Zero Fighter, by Masatake Okumiya, Jiro Horikoshi and Martin Caidin, London, 1958.

Incredible Victory, by Walter Lord, New York, 1966.

Midway, by Mitsuo Fuchida and Masatake Okumiya, Annapolis, 1955.

Japanese Destroyer Captain, by Tameichi Hara, Fred Saito and Roger Pineau, New York, 1961.

Secret Missions, by Ellis M. Zacharias, New York, 1946.

The U.S. Army in World War II: The War in the Pacific, by Louis Morton, Washington, 1962.

History of Marine Corps Aviation in World War II, by Robert Sherrod, Washington, 1952.

The Army Air Forces in World War II, Vol. 4 by W. F. Craven and J. L. Cate, Chicago, 1950.

History of United States Naval Operations in World War II, Vol. 6, by Samuel Eliot Morison, Boston, 1950.

But Not in Shame, by John Toland, New York, 1961.

The Broken Seal, by Ladislas Farago, New York, 1967.

The Code-Breakers, by David Kahn, New York, 1967.

I am also indebted to my secretary, Miss Elsie George, to Carlisle H. Humelsine and Donald J. Gonzales of Colonial Williamsburg, to my wife, Evangeline, and to my editor of long standing, Robert D. Loomis.

Burke Davis

Williamsburg, Virginia

Chapter Notes

Chapter 1

THE DECISION OF ADMIRAL NIMITZ to order Yamamoto's death is based on an account given to the author by Admiral E. T. Layton. Details of the setting in Nimitz's office were drawn from *Life*, July 10, 1944, and *The New Yorker*, June 20, 1942. Also consulted was *The Great Sea War*, by E. B. Potter and Chester W. Nitmitz.

The intercepted message which led to the assassination was taken from Eiichi Sorimachi's biography of Yamamoto, as translated by Mrs. John Toland; a nearly identical version, supplied by the War History Office, National Defense College, Japan Defense Agency, appears in David Kahn's *The Code-Breakers*, p. 598. Mr. Kahn also gave advice on problems encountered in tracing the course of the message from interception to the final decision. Captain Dyer, Colonel Lasswell and Admiral Layton, who read this section, made helpful comments.

The account of Washington's role in the mission is based on the recollections of former Intelligence operatives, Captain Charles N. Spinks and Ladislas Farago, on Admiral Morison's statement in his *History of U.S. Naval Operations in World War II*, Vol. 6, p. 128, and on testimony from Admiral Mott, who was stationed in the White House Map Room. President Roosevelt's whereabouts were determined from records at the FDR Library, Hyde Park, New York.

An example of the mythology of the mission is to be found in John D. Potter's biography of Yamamoto, p. 302, where there is a colorful but inaccurate version of the role of Secretary Knox; Charles Lindbergh is the authority for the statement that he (Lindbergh) took no part in the decision.

Naval Intelligence files which might have clarified the

intricate processes of interception, decoding, translation and decision-making were not available to the author. For example, Naval History reported that it was unable to locate files of the Fleet Radio Unit, Pacific. The writer was furnished the war diary of COMAIRSOPAC for the period.

The message, Halsey to Mitscher, on p. 13, is taken from a copy in the personal files of Lieutenant General Henry Viccellic, U.S.A.F., Ret.

Chapter 2

THIS SKETCH of the career and personality of Yamamoto is drawn chiefly from the biographies in Japanese by Agawa and Sorimachi; the latter, making use of the recollections of Admiral Fukudome, an eyewitness, gave a full description of the scene as Yamamoto awaited word from the attack on Pearl Harbor, p. 455 ff. Added details are drawn from Captain Watanabe's account, cited by Sorimachi, Walter Lord's *Incredible Victory*, and from Potter's *Yamamoto*.

Yamamoto's career as a spy and naval attaché in Washington is described by Captain Ellis Zacharias in *Secret Missions*, p. 91 ff.

The account of Yamamoto's role at the London Naval Conference is from Agawa, p. 28 ff.

The celebrated remark of Yamamoto to Prince Konoye, forecasting early Japanese victories and eventual defeat, is cited in Konoye's memoirs in *Asohi Shimbun*, pp. 20–31.

The alleged affair between Yamamoto and the geisha Chioko Kawai became the subject of controversy in Japan after publication of Agawa's book. This narrative accepts Agawa's version, though it differs in detail from those offered by others, including Sorimachi, Potter and Walter Lord in *Incredible Victory*.

This version of the evolution of Yamamoto's Pearl Harbor plan is based chiefly on Ladislas Farago's *The Broken Seal*, p. 128 ff. (an account based in part on interviews with the participants, Yasuji Watanabe, Minoru Genda and Osomi Nagano, and on depositions made at their postwar trial by Genda, Ryunosuke Kusaka and Mitsuo Fuchida). John Toland, who interviewed many of the principals in preparation of his forthcoming history of the Japanese war effort, also made valuable suggestions. Other sources: James A. Field, Jr., "Admiral Yamamoto," *U.S. Naval Institute Pro-*

ceedings, Vol. 75, No. 10, p. 1105 ff.; Admiral Fukudome, "Hawaii Operation," USNIP, Vol. 81, No. 12, p. 315 ff.; *Japanese Destroyer Captain*, by Tamechi Hara, pp. 43–44. Agawa and Sorimachi also offer accounts of this key phase of Yamamoto's career.

This brief description of Admiral Nagumo's approach to Pearl Harbor is based on Lord's *A Day of Infamy* and Toland's *But Not in Shame*, and the reception of the news of the attack is drawn from Sorimachi, p. 455 ff. Captain Watanabe's version of Yamamoto's response to America's angry reaction at the news of Pearl Harbor is given in Agawa, p. 309.

Chapter 3

THIS ACCOUNT OF THE LEADING PILOTS of the mission during the opening days of the war is based on interviews and correspondence with each of them, and with their commander, Lieutenant General Viccellio. Besby F. Holmes published a brief version of his recollections of Pearl Harbor Day in *Popular Aviation*, March/April, 1967. Added details of the contemporary San Francisco scene were taken from the city's newspapers, the *Chronicle*, *Call-Bulletin* and *Examiner*. I am indebted to Mrs. Margaret Sanborn of Mill Valley, California, for this research. Also consulted: *The History of the 70th Fighter Squadron, 13th Air Force*, typescript, Aerospace Studies Institute, Maxwell Air Force Base, Alabama.

Chapter 4

YAMAMOTO'S POST-PEARL HARBOR PROBLEMS are graphically described by Sorimachi, p. 480 ff., by Lord in *Incredible Victory*, and in Potter's *Yamamoto*, pp. 129 and 139.

Emperor Hirohito's victory message to Yamamoto is cited by Potter, p. 125; glimpses of life aboard the *Yamato* in those days are given by Agawa in his introduction and by Lord throughout the opening sections of *Incredible Victory*.

Yamamoto's letter to his sister on p. 61 is cited by Sorimachi, p. 498.

The development of the Midway Plan is fully told by Lord, by John Toland in *But Not in Shame*, by Sorimachi through the recollections of Admiral Fukudome, and from other Japanese points of view by Mitsuo Fuchida and Masa-take Okumiya in their *Midway, the Battle That Doomed Japan*.

The summary of the Doolittle raid is based on *Thirty Seconds over Tokyo*, by Ted Lawson, Theodore Taylor's *The Magnificent Mitscher*, and on Fuchida and Okumiya in *Midway*.

The story of Midway, as told here with brevity, and largely from Yamamoto's viewpoint, owes much to authors of well-known works, and especially to Fuchida and Okumiya, Lord Potter and Toland.

Yamamoto's misconception of American intentions on Guadalcanal, based on faulty information from Captain Watanabe, is described by Field in USNIP, October—December, 1940, p. 1111.

The Admiral's pessimistic outlook as revealed at Truk in late summer, 1942, is based on Sorimachi, p. 480, citing a letter of August 28 to an unknown correspondent. Goro Takase's testimony is drawn from the same source, p. 482.

Yamamoto's cheerless letter to Shimizu (p. 72) appears in Potter, p. 300.

Chapter 5

VICCELLIO AND HIS PILOTS furnished recollections of their days on the Fijis, New Caledonia and Guadalcanal.

Memories of the pilots were corroborated by press releases for various dates of 1943 issued by the 13th Fighter Command, now on file at Maxwell Air Force Base, and in many instances by citations accompanying decorations—as in the cases of Lanphier, Barber, Jacobson, Canning, Rivers and Joe Moore.

Chapter 6

GENERAL IMAMURA'S REPORT on Yamamoto's outlook during the struggle for the Solomons is cited by Sorimachi, p. 498 ff.

A summary of the I Operation from Japanese sources, by Hattori Takushiro, is in the Historical Manuscript File of the Office of the Chief of Military History, U.S. Army; a copy is in the author's collection. Other versions of this offensive were found in Agawa and Sorimachi, and in American histories of the war in the South Pacific, especially *The Army Air Forces in World War II*, Vol. 4, Wesley F. Craven and James L. Cate, eds. pp. 47–93; *History of Marine Corps Aviation in World War II* by Robert Sherrod, pp. 98–142; and *The U.S. Army in World War II. The War in the Pacific . . . the First Two Years* by Louis Morton, pp. 324–51.

The two Japanese biographies also detail Yamamoto's last days on Rabaul. Sorimachi cited the recollections of Fukudome, Yoshio Miwa, Kusaka, Joshima and Watanabe, and Agawa recounted the futile warnings by Imamura. In correspondence with the author, Watanabe described the *shogi* game of Yamamoto's last night, but said he did not recall Joshima's prophetic admonition to the Commander in Chief.

Chapter 7

ADMIRAL MITSCHER'S EARLY DAYS on Guadalcanal and the sketch of his career and personality are drawn from Taylor's biography and the recollections of pilots, including Viccellio and Sam Moore.

A copy of Halsey's message of congratulations to Viccellio's pilot who bombed a Japanese freighter with their drop tanks is in the files of Douglas Canning; Viccellio, Lanphier, Canning and Barber recalled details of the action.

A U.S. version of Yamamoto's I Operation was located in a COMAIRSOPAC Intelligence Bulletin of April 8, 1943, with an account of the deadly work of Lanphier, Barber, Moore and McLanahan. Their success in this action led to their choice as the killers of the Yamamoto mission.

In addition to the Air Corps pilots and Viccellio, Colonel Sam Moore and Admiral William A. Read, both participants, described for the author the planning process of the mission of April 18, 1943. Lanphier and Mitchell described the final Headquarters briefing during which they were assigned to the flight. Lanphier subsequently published his recollections of the mission in syndicated newspaper articles. The writer relied upon Lanphier's memory as to the contents of the message from Secretary Knox which ordered the assassination—a version published in *The Reader's Digest*, December, 1966, p. 84. A variation appears in Potter's *Yamamoto*, p. 304.

The writer was unable to resolve one conflict of testimony

concerning the sequence of events in the interception. General Viccellio recalls that word of the Admiral's itinerary came to Guadalcanal before April 1, perhaps as early as March 15, and that preliminary plans were laid well in advance. Other sources, Japanese and American, official and unofficial, date the intercepted message April 13—leaving five days for decoding, translation, command decision and field preparation. No documents to support General Viccellio's recollection have been found.

There are other minor discrepancies in the memories of participants as to how the flight plan was developed. Mitchell recalls that he planned the trip from start to finish; Sam Moore recalls that he and John Condon made major contributions; and Viccellio remembers that Joe McGuigan aided with his slide rule.

The final version of the plan, in any event, was the work of Mitchell, and he bore responsibilty for its accuracy in concept as well as in execution. (Previously published versions of the course are inaccurate; among other things, they ignore the magnetic variation from true north in the area, which averages about eight degrees east over the course.) Several of the pilots, including Mitchell and Barber, retain copies of the flight plan—or a list of the headings flown; the strip maps apparently did not survive. Admiral Read still owns the original map of Yamamoto's projected course which he drew at Mitscher's request.

The author was unable to identify the bomber pilots who flew the extra gas tanks from Port Moresby to Guadalcanal at the last moment. General George Kenney, who then commanded the 5th Air Force, said his records revealed only that the tanks were delivered by men of the 90th Bombardment Group.

Chapter 8

THE TAKEOFF OF THE MISSION was vividly recalled by several pilots, whose versions differed in some details. Jacobson, for example, remembered that the planes formed up over a small island nearby (probably Savo), circling there rather than above the field to frustrate Japanese spotters in the hills. Other pilots insisted that the flight formed over the fighter strip.

Some previous accounts have reported erroneously that Jim

McLanahan's plane burned as it veered from the runway after blowing a tire; the testimony of one pilot that McLanahan was forced off the strip by another plane could not be substantiated.

There is also disagreement as to how the killer section was finally formed. Lanphier and Mitchell recall that Holmes and Hine were motioned forward as alternates by Mitchell; Holmes recalls that Lanphier failed to keep his assigned position and wandered along the flight pattern until Mitchell signaled Holmes and Hine to fly foward and herd Lanphier into position. The text disregards this minor controversy.

The diagram on page 99 is believed to be an accurate representation of the leading sections of the mission, which included all pilots who are known to have been engaged, or even to have fired a shot. The exact composition of the two following sections is unknown.

Mitchell was unable to recall the identity of the pilot who so narrowly escaped a plunge into the sea during early moments of the flight.

Yamamoto's movement on the morning of April 18 were described by Admiral Ugaki in his diary, from the time they breakfasted together at about 5:30; the diary is the sole existing Japanese document describing Yamamoto's last hours and death. Though the diary seems accurate, it contains a few errors—for one thing, Ugaki counted nine Zeroes in the escort, though all other sources, Japanese and American, put the number of fighters at six. Masatake Okumiya, in correspondence with Martin Caidin, said that only six fighters and two bombers left Rabaul, and that he personally "sent them off."

There is agreement among surviving participants that it was Canning who first saw the Yamamoto planes and broke radio silence to announce them—but the pilots do not agree as to how far away the enemy were when sighted. Estimates of the distance range from three to ten miles. The discrepancies in the pilots' versions of the appearance of the Japanese planes are typical of varied impressions reported by men in swift aerial combat.

Chapter 9

THIS NARRATIVE of the brief combat over Bougainville is told entirely from the viewpoints of participants, often in their own words. No attempt was made to resolve inconsistencies or conflicts of testimony by editing each pilot's version. Each American flier involved in the fighting gave his story by interview and correspondence, and the narrative preserves the fact and spirit of each man's version. Because the pilots saw the action in this way, and could not then have known who had shot down Yamamoto, the text had merely combined their narratives as they reflect their impressions at the time. However, these versions were interpreted in their relationship to one another by the author in a search for a consistent pattern and in an effort to relate them individually and collectively to what now appear to be the facts.

Uncertainty as to who shot down the second bomber over the sea provides a strikingly similar case to that of the first bomber. Air Force historians have made no comprehensive search for evidence which might resolve these controversies.

From the Japanese side, all the action is seen through the eyes of Ugaki.

The first participant to publish his version of the mission was Lanphier, in 1945. Though Mitchell and Barber sought, in vain, to have the record changed by correspondence with Air Force historians, other pilots remained silent until Besby F. Holmes published his version in *Popular Aviation* in 1967 —a version with which Mitchell and Barber also disagreed.

Chapter 10

THOUGH THERE IS no truly clarifying and definitive document on the Yamamoto mission, official sources (all in Aerospace Studies Institute, Maxwell Air Force Base, Alabama) are plentiful. The following, listed chronologically, are based on accounts of returning pilots, as described in this chapter:

Daily Log, 347th Fighter Group, 18 Apr. 43.
Intelligence Bulletin, COMAIRSOLS, 18 Apr. 43
Radiogram COMDR 3rd Fleet—COMAIRSOLS, 18 Apr. 43.
Air Information Bulletin, 19 Apr. 43.
Fighter Interception Report, Hq. USAFISPA 21 Apr. 43.
Combat Report, COMAIRSOLS, 21 Apr. 43.
Combat Report, COM SO PAC, 26 Apr. 43.
Other documents:
Air Diary, Aircraft SOPAC, PAC FLEET, 18 Apr. 43.

Squadron Diary, 70th Fighter Squadron.

Histories: 12th, 70th and 339th Fighter Squadrons.

Interviews by Intelligence officers with Mitchell and Lanphier, June 15 and 18, 1943, after their return to the
U.S.

Without exception these documents reflect the contemporary misconception that three Japanese bombers were shot
down on the mission.

Lieutenant John F. Kennedy's presence at the fighter strip
is noted in Robert J. Donovan's *PT-109*, P. 58. Donovan, on
the basis of testimony by one of Kennedy's crew, reported
that Lanphier did barrel rolls over the field as he returned;
the author has concluded that the stunting pilot (also observed by Admiral William A. Read of Mitscher's staff) was
one of the 12th Squadron.

Barber and Holmes, and to a lesser extent Mitchell, recall
extended arguments over credits for kills on the mission.
Since conflicts of testimony could not be resolved, these have
been dismissed with brief mention. Barber presented his
views to Air Force historians between 1947 and 1953, and
challenged the official credits, to no avail.

Ray Hine was the only U.S. casualty of the mission, but
Gordon Whittaker was killed less than two weeks later on a
strike against Bougainville, and Eldon Stratton was killed
near Vella Lavella on August 30, 1943. Albert Long died in
1950 and William Smith in 1958, both as civilians.

Viccellio recalled Mitscher's visit to the command post.
Lanphier and Read recalled other post-mission details. The
scene at Halsey's headquarters is described in *Admiral
Halsey's Story*, by Halsey and J. Bryan III, p. 155.

Mitscher's radiogram reporting success on the mission is
cited in Taylor's *The Magnificent Mitscher*, page 152.

The Air Force Film Depository, Wright-Patterson Air
Force Base, has a reel of film showing the mission's pilots
posing for an awards ceremony on April 19, 1943.

Mack Morriss, of Elizabethton, Tennessee, kindly supplied
notes from his diary detailing conditions near Henderson
Field during the night after the mission.

Chapter 11

THE BIOGRAPHERS SORIMACHI AND AGAWA published
full narratives of the search for Yamamoto's body, its crema-

tion, and the funerals in Japan. Potter added graphic details from undisclosed sources.

The official Japanese report on the Admiral's death, furnished by Colonel Nishiura of the Japan Defense Agency, and previously unpublished:

Secret Telegram: No. 181430 (1943.4.18)

From: The Commander, South Eastern Area
Fleet and Air Arm.

To: The Minister of the Navy,
The Commander in Chief.

The two Riku-ko and six Choku-an fighter planes carrying (the staffs of) the Combined Fleet Headquarters encountered enemy fighter planes, ten plus in number, at 0740 (07:40) over Buin today and engaged them in an air battle. The No. 1 Riku-ko (carrying the Director, the Surgeon Commander, Staff Officer Okezumi, the Assistant Director) on fire fell into the midst of a jungle 11 miles West of Buin in a shallow angle. The No. 2 Riku-ko (carrying the Chief Staff Officer, the Chief Paymaster, the Chief Meteorological and Operational Officer, and Staff Officer Muroi) made a forced landing in the sea, South of Moila. It is known, at present, that only the Chief Staff Officer and the Chief Paymaster (both of them wounded) were rescued. The rescue forces are at work at present.

Okumiya's description of Admiral Kakuda's reaction as word of the tragedy reached the fleet appears in *Zero*, pp. 245–46 and 254.

The radio announcement by which the Japanese people learned of Yamamoto's death was reported by Field in *USNIP*, October–December, 1949, p. 1111.

The contention that one urn of Yamamoto's ashes was delivered to the geisha Chioko Kawai is offered in Agawa, p. 324.

Sorimachi's biography contains photographs of the Yamamoto shrine, gravestones and monument.

Epilogue

Mitchell, Barber and Jacobson described the scene in General Harmon's office on or shortly after April 23, 1943. The date of the flight from Guadalcanal was noted by Mack Morriss in his diary. Lanphier has a copy of the Harmon–Arnold letter reporting on the mission.

Admiral Ugaki's final flight is described by William Craig in *The Fall of Japan,* pp. 215–16.

ABOUT THE AUTHOR

BURKE DAVIS traveled extensively in the course of researching *GET YAMAMOTO*. He interviewed every American who fired a shot on the mission, plus dozens more. From historians and biographers in Japan he gathered new material about Yamamoto never before published in the United States. Mr. Davis is the author of four biographies—including *The Billy Mitchell Affair*—several military histories, and four novels. He lives in Williamsburg, Virginia.

BANTAM BESTSELLERS

OUTSTANDING BOOKS NOW AVAILABLE
AT A FRACTION
OF THEIR ORIGINAL COST!